THE ENTREPRENEURIAL NONPROFIT EXECUTIVE

THE ENTREPRENEURIAL NONPROFIT EXECUTIVE

THOMAS A. McLAUGHLIN

FUND RAISING INSTITUTE
A Division of the Taft Group
Rockville, Maryland

Published by
Fund Raising Institute
A Division of The Taft Group
12300 Twinbrook Parkway, Suite 450
Rockville, Maryland 20852
(301) 816-0210

Printed in the United States of America

96   95   94   93   92   91   6   5   4   3   2   1

Library of Congress Catalog Card Number: 91-071517
ISBN 0-930807-22-7

Fund Raising Institute publishes books on fund raising, philanthropy, and
nonprofit management. To request sales information, or a copy of our catalog,
please write us at the above address or call 1-800-877-TAFT.

CONTENTS

III. The People

IV. Appendix

ACKNOWLEDGMENTS

Many people helped, directly or indirectly, with the writing of this book. An incalculable number helped me write some of this material even though neither of us realized it at the time, and I realized it only later. These people are too numerous to mention; I can only hope they recognize some of their ideas or actions in the pages that follow.

As to those whom I can thank explicitly, Yitzhak Bakal was the first person to introduce me to many of the ideas I have struggled to present here. Cathy Dunham gave me the chance to pursue many of them in sometimes unorthodox form, and John Mc-Manus sustained it after her. For recognizing an opportunity, I am indebted to Peter Nessen, and to Tom Spence and Dennis Fusco for their unfailing support in the pursuit of it. Jim Aldrich provided many thoughtful comments on my ideas, as did Adrian Becher. Chuck Lean has been consistent, skilled and knowledgeable throughout the entire process of producing this book.

Most important of all, I want to thank my wife, Gail Sendecke and my children, Paul and Emily Rose, for allowing me to spend on this project so much of the time I should have been spending with them.

INTRODUCTION

The average nonprofit executive is expected to have a desire to do vast numbers of good works, an aversion to things financial, and a deep and abiding respect for the inherent limitations of the nonprofit form of business organization.

In short, the average nonprofit executive is expected to fail.

The hidden truth of nonprofit management is that the rules—whether they are actual government-issued regulations, philanthropy guidelines, or simply the "rules" of long-standing tradition—work against success for most nonprofit executives. The reasons for this are multiple and complicated and range from simple policymaker inattention to frank resistance to the nonprofit form of business.

I consider myself a nonprofit executive at heart. I like nonprofit organizations. For nearly two decades I have worked for them, managed them, consulted with them, and lobbied on their behalf. Until relatively recently, I had never even taken a paycheck from a company which had as one of its purposes the creation of wealth in private hands. And during that time the most successful nonprofit executives I have encountered have had one thing in common: *they ignored the "rules" and instead sought out opportunities for their organizations.* Whether it was instinct or studied response, they refused to accept the many limitations ready to be imposed on them and instead created situation after situation for the people they served (and those who worked for them) to gain something of value. In short, they were entrepreneurial nonprofit executives.

"Nonprofit" is a terrible term. The only thing it should signify is that an organization has no shareholders in the Wall Street sense of the word. Instead, it has taken on endless connotations, few of them organizationally or financially healthy. The entrepreneurial nonprofit executive understands this and is not afraid to challenge conventional thinking.

In the past decade, as government funding diminished and philanthropy failed to make up the difference, many nonprofit organizations have started to plan for-profit ventures of one sort or another. That this is happening at all is ironic, since it implies that some or all of the services offered by a group from some point forward are intended to be carried out for profit, whereas all those that had gone before were not.

Judging from my years of practice and observation, the only successful way out of this dilemma is to run the nonprofit organization as though it were any other entrepreneurial venture; in short, the solution is to become an entrepreneurial nonprofit executive.

Those who pick up this book hoping to learn, say, how a mental health clinic can sell employee assistance programs to private industry or how a museum can profitably run a souvenir store will be disappointed. Being an entrepreneurial nonprofit executive is a way of thinking, an attitude of prudent risk-taking in the service of a larger mission. It has nothing to do with the subtleties of the Internal Revenue Service code. Success as an entrepreneurial nonprofit executive cannot be measured solely by the results on a balance sheet nor by the size or complexity of the organization developed, although these are inescapable elements. Rather, the entrepreneurial nonprofit executive judges himself—and is judged by others—according to the success by which he or she fulfills the organizational mission through the creation of a responsive, viable, and lasting organization.

I have gathered the material for this book over the course of many years. Although I did not explicitly interview any executive director for this book, it is based on my work with and for literally hundreds of nonprofit executives of agencies ranging from the very smallest up to those with yearly budgets measured in the tens of millions of dollars. Wherever possible, I have avoided using any individuals' or agencies' names as examples of either good or bad management. Rest assured that there is no single nonprofit entrepreneurial executive model sitting quietly in his office waiting to be discovered. Instead, I have tried to describe a style and an attitude that virtually anyone can strive to emulate.

And that is truly the central point of this book. Not everyone can be the epitome of the entrepreneurial nonprofit executive, nor should he or she. But everyone charged with nonprofit management responsibilities can and should understand the ways in which he or she can use that position with energy and creativity to further the mission through the creation of opportunity. While this book is unlikely to dramatically reshape any one executive's approach, I do hope it will occasionally stimulate a new way of looking at the task. And in a society where many for-profit companies are asked to do nothing more significant than to manufacture lilac-scented air freshener or toaster-ready frozen waffles while nonprofits are expected to protect children, care for the sick, and preserve our cultures, the stakes are high enough to warrant the effort.

PART I

THE MYTHS

CHAPTER 1

MYTH #1: WE SHOULDN'T MAKE A PROFIT

See that door over there? The one marked "Tax-Exempt Organizations"? Open it. Go ahead, swing it wide open. There's plenty of room on the other side.

There. Now step inside, there are a lot of things I'd like to show you.

Start with those hospital buildings right in front of you. And the university complex, the art museum, the scientific institute, the religious group, and the day-care center. Familiar enough. But if you look hard, you'll see some places you may not have thought much about, like battered women's shelters and community development corporations and hospices. These are all tax-exempt organizations, and they are also usually public charities, because not only are they organized for religious, charitable, scientific, educational, or other similar purposes, they get most of their revenue in one way or another from the general public.

Most of the time, we say an organization is nonprofit when what we really mean is that it's a nonprofit public charity. There are lots of other groups that are nonprofit, but they're not public charities. Private foundations, for example, often seem to the casual observer to be public charities, but owing to their typically restricted revenue sources the government considers them a separate class altogether.

Look to your right for an example of a group that's nonprofit but not a charity: chambers of commerce. Also real estate boards

3

and boards of trade. That sports club of yours that you recognize in the back is nonprofit, and so is the fraternal club you joined last year.

Wait, it gets more interesting. See that cluster of health insurance plans over there? Those are voluntary employees' beneficiary associations. Never heard of them? Look closely, there's a fair chance that you or a friend or neighbor get your health insurance through a VEBA without realizing it.

Here the telephones ringing? Mutual telephone companies are nonprofit. Credit unions and cemetery companies find a place in the nonprofit tax code too. And look way back there in the corner, but blow the coal dust off first. Okay, now read it—black lung benefits trusts are nonprofit organizations.

This room just seems to stretch on, doesn't it? Amateur sports organizations are nonprofit, as are religious and apostolic associations. Teachers' retirement fund associations, veterans' organizations, group legal services plans, etc. But you get the picture. What all of these groups have in common is that the federal government is willing to forgo applying a tax to their main business.

You can leave the door open. No one in here is eager to leave. Especially in these days of revenue-hungry governments, it's remarkable that public policymakers continue to give up any chance of taxing these corporations. Since the ability of most nonprofits to hire lobbying help to defend their interests is limited, this situation must say something about the value society places on these groups' work. Perhaps that is why admission into this room is not automatic, the Internal Revenue Service having decided that every new business entity is for-profit until proven otherwise. And there are some special rules that apply whenever one of these groups decides to go out of business.

But other than that, corporations certified exempt from federal tax are still business entities subject to the same uncertainties of the economy at large and having to solve most of the same internal management riddles as their for-profit counterparts. In fact, I will argue later on that their management assignment is even tougher than that of their sister corporations, though it doesn't necessarily have to be. Anyway, the point is that in spite of their preferential tax treatment they are still businesses and have to act like ones if they want to accomplish what they set out to do.

Which is why "nonprofit" is a terrible term. At the very least, it clouds the real nature of these organizations by suggesting images of pleasant ladies with blue hair presiding over garden clubs with shoebox financial records. For those firmly committed to the pursuit of profit it signals that there is something second-rate and impossible to understand about those not similarly committed. On the other side, for the uninitiated in the nonprofit field it can seem to confirm what they thought all along about the dirtiness of the very idea of profit. In short, it does more harm than good.

"Tax-exempt" is a far better, more accurate term. All it means is that the profits of the organization cannot be distributed to the organization's shareholders—because tax-exempt organizations can have no shareholders. In a very real sense, the general public can be viewed as the "owner" of tax-exempt corporations, a kind of structural quid pro quo for having given up the opportunity to tax. Unhappily, the term nonprofit has stuck, so until the collective consciousness gets raised a few more notches, we'll continue to see the word "nonprofit" used where "tax-exempt" would probably be more accurate—like in the title of this book, for example.

Here's another bit of damage done by the conventional associations with the term "nonprofit." People in the field, especially those less familiar with the plain facts of tax-exempt matters, tend to use the term to mean far more than it really does. In one meaning, "But we're nonprofit" is code for being small, powerless, and out of the economic mainstream.

Let's analyze that notion.

In 1987, this country's 907,000 nonprofit public charities spent *$261.5 billion* on their various operations, an amount roughly equivalent to one-quarter of the entire federal budget and 5.8 percent of the total national income. Add in all other tax-exempt organizations and you come up to 6.5 percent of total national income. Excluding volunteers, public charities employed 7.4 million people, or 6 percent of the entire work force. Overall, public charities have consistently represented about 4 percent of the total number of institutions in the United States over the past ten years.

Does this sound like small potatoes to you?

The most insidious incidence of the "We Shouldn't Make a Profit" myth is found in nonprofit staff themselves. Typically it takes one of two forms. The first is tinged with overtones of moral superiority, the second with a sigh of resignation. Both start the same way. "We're nonprofit [so we're superior to the profit-grubbers]" goes one chant. The other explains why something wasn't done. "We're nonprofit, so we can't. . . ." Let's take them separately.

For the self-appointed guardians of the collective moral fiber, try this exercise. Ask a group of staff to list on a blackboard all of the qualities they associate with for-profit business in a financial management context (the exercise works equally well with board members too). Make it clear that there is no "right" or "wrong" answer, that this is an exercise in analyzing connotations. Chances are, you will get a list that looks something like this one, a product of a recent training session I did incorporating this exercise:

For-Profit Business

Big
Organized
Good public image
Humanity secondary
Marketing
Overrate their competition
Bottom line
Stockholders
Controlled

Now go through the same process to develop a set of connotations associated with nonprofit organizations. Again, you will probably get a list that looks similar to this one:

For-Profit Business	Nonprofit Business
Big	Struggling
Organized	Low salary/high turnover
Good public image	Human service-oriented
Humanity secondary	Community-focused
Marketing	Tax-deductible donations
Overrate their competition	Humane
Bottom line	Volunteers
Stockholders	Poor employee benefits
Controlled	

Now for the fun part. Ask staff to evaluate each of these connotations one by one using two simple rules. If the condition has to be true by law for that type of business entity, leave it there. Otherwise, erase it. Erase it also if it has to be true for that type of business entity but also has to be true by law for the other type. Using the above chart as an example, here is what you are left with:

For-Profit Business	Nonprofit Business
Stockholders	Tax-deductible donations

This is the short list of inescapable differences between nonprofit and for-profit business organizations. By now, the message should be clear that nonprofit organizations are capable of exactly the same things, good and bad, as for-profit businesses, and that the necessary differences are rather uninterestingly technical in nature. To the extent that they exist at all, claims on the moral high ground derive from the people and the mission, not from the type of business organization the corporate vehicle happens to use.

The other form of myth to find voice in this phrase comes as a sigh of resignation, as in "I'd like to purchase better furniture for the waiting room, but we're nonprofit. . . ." This one gives me shivers just writing it. Normally you hear it from entry-level staff or new board members. Accompanied by either a literal or figurative shrug, it is intended to elicit sympathy and understanding for the speaker's or agency's presumed plight. What it really does is seek permission to avoid further (or better) accomplishment.

My response is polite, restrained, and subtle. *WHAT IN HELL DOES YOUR EMPLOYER'S TAX STATUS HAVE TO DO WITH YOUR PURCHASING DECISIONS???* If a product or a service is necessary to deliver the performance that one is employed to deliver, then the responsible employee has an obligation at least to seek that product or service. Let it be denied due to management's professional difference of opinion, or because there's not enough cash on hand right now, or because someone up the line doesn't like the color of the upholstery proposed. But don't let it be denied on the basis of the agency's tax status and all that that's presumed to imply.

Now if the speaker truly is a new employee the roar might be toned down a bit so as not to wipe out a future star. But there should be no mistaking the essence of the message. Being a nonprofit organization is a form of tax status, and it neither can nor should have anything to do with any policy or procedure of the corporation.

Look at it this way. If you did the math earlier when I cited 907,000 nonprofit public charities employing 7.4 million people, you found that the average number of full-time staff per corporation was a shade over eight. If the so-called average nonprofit corporation were a for-profit business with those dimensions, it is likely that it would be something called a "Subchapter S" corporation, a tax status that many small businesses choose. What do you think the chances are that someone at this precise moment is sitting around saying "Well, I'd like to buy that new lathe, but we're a Subchapter S corporation . . ."?

Give yourself and your agency a break. Shed the old notions of what it means to be nonprofit and you'll feel an unmistakable sense of liberation.

CHAPTER 2

MYTH #2: WE DON'T NEED TO MAKE A PROFIT

Now that we have established the permissibility, moral and otherwise, of a nonprofit corporation making a profit, the entirely sensible question you may have is *why?* Why would a nonprofit organization want to make a profit if it has no shareholders to whom it could pass it along? The answer is simple: for almost all the same reasons that any for-profit corporation wants to make a profit. Let's look at some of them.

Growth

Perhaps the most obvious reason why the entrepreneurial nonprofit manager would want a yearly profit is so that organization will grow. Almost always, achieving the kind of growth that's measurable in dollars (we'll get to the other kind of growth later) means the agency must first put out some money of its own. Nonprofit corporations are at a distinct disadvantage compared to their for-profit brethren in this respect, since the latter can always sell some sort of ownership stake to raise money for growth whereas nonprofits usually have to rely on internally generated sources of growth capital. True, public charities are eligible for foundation grants, but you might want to check out the later chapter on this subject before you start betting on grants for growth.

To understand how growth can come about through profits,

9

look at the chart below. It assumes that each of two nonprofit corporations starts out with five thousand dollars in cash, and the same amount owed to suppliers. Agency A breaks even each year. Agency B, however, is run entrepreneurially and shows a $30,000 profit at the end of year one, which it immediately uses to purchase a building for one hundred fifty thousand dollars with 20 percent down.

Assuming the same pattern of revenue, expenses, and profit hold true for years two and three, Agency B is in a very good position for operations growth during year four. Most new programming requires at least minimal funding for the start-up phase, and Agency B can raise that cash in several different ways. It can set aside a bit of its cash (though it may find doing so difficult, considering that it has less than 10 percent of the cash it needs to pay its yearly expenses on hand). It can also borrow

The Effect of Yearly Profits on Non-Profit Corporations

Revenue and Expense Statement

	Year One		Year Two		Year Three	
	A	B	A	B	A	B
Revenue	$750,000	$750,000	$750,000	$750,000	$750,000	$750,000
Expenses	$750,000	$720,000	$750,000	$720,000	$750,000	$720,000
Profit	$0	$30,000	$0	$30,000	$0	$30,000

Balance Sheet

	Year One		Year Two		Year Three	
	A	B	A	B	A	B
ASSETS						
Cash	$5,000	$35,000	$5,000	$35,000	$5,000	$65,000
Building	—	—	—	$150,000	—	$150,000
TOTAL ASSETS	$5,000	$35,000	$5,000	$185,000	$5,000	$215,000
LIABILITIES						
Payables	$5,000	$5,000	$5,000	$5,000	$5,000	$5,000
Mortgage	—	—	—	$120,000	—	$120,000
EQUITIES						
Fund Balance		$30,000		$60,000		$90,000
TOTAL LIABILITIES AND FUND BALANCE	$5,000	$35,000	$5,000	$185,000	$5,000	$215,000

against its equity in the building and charge the interest payments against the new program. If necessary it can sell the building to raise the necessary cash. And whatever it does, it also can enjoy the full benefit of whatever appreciation the building may have undergone in the two years Agency B owned it.

Agency A has no such options. It has barely enough cash to make it from day to day, it owns nothing of value, and its fund balance is pitiful. The only real option Agency A has in order to raise funds for growth is to postpone paying some of the bills it owes. But with the majority of its expenses almost certainly going to payroll, this option is severely limited. Agency A is growing nowhere.

Stability

Turning a regular profit also helps maintain stability in tough times. Let's suppose that a funding source delayed making one of its regular payments and both agencies needed to come up with $20,000 quickly in order to meet the next payroll. Which agency would you rather work for under these circumstances?

Innovation

The most effective barrier to nonprofit innovation is not psychological or organizational, it's a lack of adequate resources. Again, profitability can help. The essence of innovation is setting aside an amount of money for the purpose of carrying out an experiment. It's a kind of legalized gambling, since the entrepreneurial manager must be prepared to lose the entire amount and end up with nothing to show for it. What better place to find a few dollars for this worthy purpose than profits? And it will often be possible to earn back some or all of the profit-generated seed money if the project is successful, so that you have effectively created a revolving fund.

Mistakes

The most underrated use of profits—in *any* organization, for-profit or nonprofit—is to bury mistakes. It's amazing how easy it is to cover today's blunders when you can expect an extra fifty or hundred thousand tomorrow. What's that you say? You think you'll go through your entire career as a nonprofit manager without making any mistakes? Or, when you do make a mistake you say you will simply fess up and fix it right away? Get real.

How Much?

Now that I have you agreeing, more or less, that this nonprofit organization of yours needs to make a profit, I will confess something. *I don't know how much profit you need to make.* I wish I could tell you that in a certain type of nonprofit corporation you need to hit 2 percent, and in another type you should aim for 5 percent. I can't. Mainly the reason for this situation is that good theorizing about profit levels in nonprofits is conspicuous by its absence (note that I'm talking about what profit levels should be, not what they *actually* are, although there isn't a whole lot more usable information on that subject either). But what I can do is to think through the situation with you.

Start with this fundamental irony. Every organization, taxable and tax-exempt, needs profits. Yet we frown on profits. You already know how the old-fashioned notion of nonprofit management frowns on profit. Well, so do taxable corporations. Sort of. You see, Uncle Sam and his various nephews in other levels of government like to tax corporate profits. That means that corporate types have an incentive to understate their net profit for tax purposes even while their owners normally like to see healthy profits. It's a dilemma, and I often wonder how my business school classmates solve it.

In any event, it might be helpful to look at how much profit other service industries normally report. The chart below shows some representative common industries' net profit margins.[1]

INDUSTRY	LOWEST AVERAGE PROFIT	HIGHEST AVERAGE PROFIT
Electric services	2.8%	11.4%
Gas stations	.2%	1.5%
Insurance agents	7.3%	16.8%
Medical laboratories	4.4%	10.3%
Wholesale car parts	.9%	3.5%
Wholesale paper products	1.3%	2.5%
Securities brokers	4.0%	18.4%
Building operators and lessors	15.3%	22.9%

(Note: figures are for companies reporting net profits.)
Source: Almanac of Business & Industrial Financial Ratios (Troy, 1990)

If there is a general theme to the industries above, it is that the lowest profit margins are found in companies dealing with commodities, while the highest margins are in fields where profit is derived from fewer and more customized transactions. (Don't equate big dollar values with lots of transactions. The focal point of a gas station transaction happens hundreds of times daily, while building operators' real transactions are their buildings under management.) Finding your agency's place on the service delivery continuum from commodity-like service to highly individualized attention can be a good first step in thinking about your desirable profit level.

While at first glance it may appear that most nonprofit organizations give highly individualized attention, many are actually more oriented to the commodity end of the scale. Museums, for instance, can be seen as commodity processors (stop grinding your teeth), since their survival depends on persuading large numbers of people to enter and survey their collections. Ordinarily, the tip-off to commodity-like operations is if the group's mission implies getting large numbers of people to pay relatively small amounts of money for identical increments of service. The larger the size of each individual transaction (defined as a use of the proffered service, not necessarily as the exchange of money), and the more unique the attention paid to the service recipient, the larger the profit margin probably should be.

Another factor to keep in mind when comparing your operations with traditional for-profit business is the effect of tax policy. Because corporate taxes are paid on net profits and because individual corporations' tax positions are unique, net profits for analytical purposes are reported before taxes are paid. Notice that the chart above is based only on companies that made a profit. For a variety of reasons, many companies do not even report a profit—in my state, more than a third of the domestic for-profit corporations reported no net profit at all. And the net profits shown in the chart will be reduced by an individual corporation's tax rate before the company gets to use any of the money anyway. Perhaps a third to a half will be lost to taxes in that way.

Finally, taxable corporations use a number of conventional means of reducing their tax liability. Accelerated depreciation schedules, based on the argument that the conventional "straight line" depreciation calculation doesn't reflect what really happens to a capital asset, boost expenses in the early years of an asset's life and thereby reduce taxes. There is relatively little use of this technique in most nonprofits. Many other accounting provisions and management policies also exist chiefly to reduce the tax bite, so it is misleading to draw exact correlations between tax-exempt and taxable enterprises. Still, a brief stroll through comparable net profit statistics can help the entrepreneurial nonprofit manager clarify his or her own situation.

How to Create a Profit

In the end, there are only two ways of creating a profit: boosting revenue or reducing expenses. Let's take reducing expenses first.

Cutting Expenses

By thinking entrepreneurially about reducing your nonprofit organization's expenses, you can take immediate savings while positioning yourself to discover future ones.

Most of the time, finding savings in a nonprofit's operations is like following a trail in the woods—you take one step at a time, and if the markers fade away so does the will to go forward. Effective cost reduction, however, requires a more systematic approach sustained over time. And to be truly worthwhile, it should be carried out with the same sense of entrepreneurialism that drives a development campaign.

There are four levels in a good entrepreneurial cost-cutting effort: (1) an industry watch; (2) a review of spending authorization patterns; (3) a review of spending patterns; and (4) an employee suggestion program. For the most part, these levels are independent of each other, so that concentrating only on that level can produce payoffs regardless of what you do on any other level. Let's look at what entrepreneurial cost-cutting entails.

Industry Watch

It has become a truism that the pace of change has quickened in the past several years. (Remember when no one owned a fax machine?) With change comes opportunity, and there is plenty of change in the American business community today that can spell opportunity for the nonprofit manager who knows how to take advantage of it.

Take the office supplies industry, for example. For many years, the individual office supplies customer and the small business were served largely by the corner stationery store, which essentially was selling two things: 1) access to a full office supply product line, often from different suppliers; and 2) convenience. In return for these services, the customer paid a relatively standard amount over the wholesale price.

Along came discount office supplies warehouses in the 1980s and the economics of the industry changed. These new entries offer an expanded product line and greatly reduced retail prices, paying for it all by vastly expanding volume. Some of their competitors have responded by stressing service over price, a classic strategy in transitions of this sort. The result is that individuals and small businesses for whom the most important consideration is price are accepting the inconvenience of greater distance in return for lower prices, while those to whom service is important (primarily medium-size and larger organizations) can opt for either price or service.

While the office supply industry changes were primarily in the product distribution system rather than in the product itself, other industries are seeing or will see changes due to factors ranging from technological innovation to methods of financing. Many of these changes will lead directly to an opportunity for cost reduction on the part of nonprofit organizations, and the entrepreneurial cost cutter will spot these trends by tapping into sources of information about business developments.

Spending Authorization Pattern Reviews

A second level on which to seek expense reductions is spending authorization patterns. Inquiries at this level attempt to answer the question, "Who has authority to spend money on behalf of the agency, and how much authority does he or she have?" Questions will range from the very biggest ("Who has authority to hire, set salaries, and give raises?") to the very smallest ("Who has access to the telephone after five o'clock?").

Throughout, the purpose is to "map" the entity's pattern of spending authorizations to see that it is compatible with organizational mission, structure, and logistics. Often it is just as important to make explicit the spending authorization patterns currently in existence. Organizations abhor a vacuum just as much as nature does, and when no stated authorization pattern is in place, a makeshift one will be created. The first step is to discern how spending really occurs *right now*.

Remedial action for skewed spending authorizations is mainly composed of realignments up, down, or sideways. That is, you need to determine the maximum spending each staff person can authorize, then make sure that the correct person at the correct level is responsible for the spending. For example, many organizations with field offices allow the people in charge to spend (according to budget) up to a certain amount per transaction. Be sure that a ceiling for one staff person is the floor for the next highest ranking staff person. And be equally sure that the spending authority is vested in the correct person at that level. Insuring that the person with the responsibility for getting the job done is also the one with spending authority is the way to do that.

Spending Pattern Review

The third level of a comprehensive expense reduction program is checking the actual content of the spending patterns. Whereas the first two levels have to do more with the process of spending, reviewing spending patterns is concerned with the actual spending itself. Primarily an analytical exercise, this review looks both inside and outside the nonprofit organization, and the overarching goal is to find natural ways of consolidating existing buying power; a secondary goal, of course, is to eliminate obviously unnecessary spending. Let's look at internal methods first.

The obvious place to start looking for economies in a labor-intensive industry such as nonprofits represent is staffing. Unhappily, this is likely to be the least productive and most dangerous area. To understand why, refer back to the spending authorization pattern review. The spending authorization pattern review seeks to answer the question, "Is this staff position necessary?"; whereas the spending pattern review asks, "Is this staff person paid at the correct level?" For most nonprofit organizations, this is an absurd question on its face, though it may occasionally be worth asking. In any event, action against the rare instances of staff overpayment is likely to cost more than it is worth.

For the nonpersonnel portion of the budget, look for ways to create larger transactions. For instance, one organization I am familiar with was able to lower its vehicle leasing costs by grouping its purchases and requesting proposals on several vehicles at once rather than one by one throughout the year. Another consolidated fuel oil purchases with a dealer willing to service several different sites as a single account because they installed larger fuel tanks at some of the locations.

Internal expense reductions must walk a fine line between centralization and decentralization, and between program effectiveness and administrative expediency. Over the years I have been involved with various networks of small residential programs that were prime candidates for a massive, centralized food and house-hold supplies buying program that would have saved megadollars. But I always refused to set one up because an important point of the programs was to give the clients in residence a chance to shop for and prepare their own food.

An inescapable fact of life for most nonprofit groups, however, is that they are usually unable to generate enough purchasing power on their own to interest reputable vendors in offering discounted prices. That's when you have to go outside the corporation to find enough similar groups to create concentrated buying power. Associations are particularly well situated to perform this service—and if there is no association ready or able to do so, it may be worth your while to create one. Always, the goal should be to create transactions large enough to harness mass buying power. There may be no such thing as a free lunch, but a hundred lunches will get you a pretty deep discount.

Employee Suggestions

Remember that your most potent sources of suggestions for cost reductions walk out the door every night. Be sure to ask your employees formally and repeatedly for their ideas on how to control costs, and be sure that they share in the payoff. A fellow I know has worked fairly unhappily for a giant utility company for 20 years, but his face positively lit up when he showed me his beeper one weekend. "See that sticker on the side of the beeper?" he asked with a big smile. "That was my idea," he said proudly. It turns out that his very commonsense suggestion for their many lost beepers was to put a sticker on the side saying "If you find this beeper, call . . .", and for his efforts he got an enthusiastic letter from the company president plus a check for $150.

It's not glamorous—in fact, systematically reducing expenses can be tedious and difficult—but it can help nonprofit managers find hidden savings and strengthen programs at a time when the odds seem against it.

Increasing Revenue

The trouble with making a profit by reducing expenses is that it is inherently regressive. Agency B created its profit by not spending money that it had presumably expected to spend. While it's fine to seize and even create opportunities to save when they arise, the fact is that pressure to forgo spending will very quickly translate into undesirable pressure on the single biggest expenditure of them all, personnel.

This is the old school style of nonprofit management, brought about because many nonprofit organizations allow themselves to operate on what amounts to fixed revenue. Did you ever wonder why for-profit corporations seem far less concerned with the cost of things than their comparably sized nonprofit counterparts? It's because an entrepreneur's solution to most financial threats is to grow. Fixed revenue streams close off that option and put a premium on cutting to survive. The entrepreneurial nonprofit manager's solution to financial threats is to unfix the revenue stream.

A clarification may be important here. For the remainder of this chapter we will deal with ways to squeeze more revenue from existing sources. A logical and, in many ways, more important approach is to develop new sources altogether. We will cover that aspect later in the book.

For many organizations, there is a powerful, virtually cost-free way to improve revenue. It is simple, elegant, and free of any moral ambivalence. It is also quite obvious. In fact, it is so obvious that if you bought this book solely to learn this tool you might want to close it right now and reopen it at a time and place where you won't be embarrassed if someone discovers that you paid all that money for something so simple. Here it is: *Follow your own rules.*

Many years ago I was hired to run a small department of a struggling YMCA. After only a few weeks I noticed that the bookkeeper smiled broadly at me whenever I came into her office, and the executive director hummed to himself a lot more. Eventually I learned that I had boosted department revenues almost 50 percent. Being a total outsider, I had simply conscientiously enforced the written pricing policies and other procedures I was given when I started. Over the years they had been allowed to slip into such a confused and arbitrary state in actual practice that just understanding and following them was enough to improve the department's yield dramatically.

Right now, while you're still thinking about it, put this book down and go test a few of your transactions. Follow them through from beginning to end. Did you charge what you said you would charge? Did the charge get recorded without errors? Was it followed up?

While you're in the neighborhood, check out the policies of those staff members governing revenue. This step is similar to the spending authorization pattern described above, in that it concentrates on those having authority to enforce your prices. I know one counseling center director who, new on the job, reluctantly decided to raise his services' prices to regain some fiscal ground, then watched in frustration as revenue stayed virtually unchanged. After some investigation, he discovered that the bookkeeper, who had been with the organization for many years, had unilaterally and with the best of intentions decided that most of their clients could not afford the new rates and was routinely waiving the increased portion of the bills. A few weeks after she finally left, revenues began climbing steadily.

If your organization offers services to the general public, it's worth making sure that your prices are competitive. And don't be afraid to raise them every year or two, rather than in a single jump after a long time. When I worked for a membership organization we went five years without a dues increase, then jacked up the membership fees to where the dues would have been had they been raised consistently just enough to cover inflation. We expected gratitude for having held off for so long. Instead, we got hammered.

Nonprofits that are heavily subsidized by one or more levels of government should be sure to stay on top of their funding source's regulatory policies 365 days a year. While routinely substantial price increases may not be feasible, funding sources usually have more flexibility than they might prefer to let on, and it is unfortunately a truism that the articulately squeaky wheel gets the grease.

Nonprofit organizations need to make profits just as much as their for-profit cousins, and for most of the same reasons. The entrepreneurial nonprofit executive knows this and acts accordingly.

CHAPTER 3

MYTH #3: WE HAVE BETTER BENEFITS

Try this test. Ask the next hundred people you meet to complete the following question about compensation in the nonprofit sector: "Sure, salaries are lower in nonprofit organizations, but _____". Can there be any doubt that 80 of them would say *"but the fringe benefits are better"?*

Ten years ago, many nonprofit administrators might have privately agreed with this assessment. Far fewer would do so today. Frankly, employee benefits in the tax-exempt field today are so tattered that it is hard to imagine how they could ever have been superior.

More likely, the better benefits myth came about as a code for more liberal employee management practices than private industry traditionally offered. Today, "fringe benefits" is one of those terms that has been so stretched through the years that it is used to mean everything from health insurance to morning coffee. Technically, it means a service provided at employer cost that doesn't affect the basic wage rate. For simplicity's sake as much as anything else, this chapter will concentrate only on benefits meeting this definition. In addition we will not cover mandated "fringe benefits," sometimes known as payroll taxes. For other aspects of personnel management, see chapter 17.

Sleepy Hamlet No More

It used to be that fringe benefits were a sleepy little hamlet in every employer's budget land. No longer. This country is entering a

23

period of relative labor scarcity, and employers of all sorts are stepping up competition for the best labor available. In fact, with the establishment of the two-income household, the expectation of flat or even declining real wages, and the aging of the baby boomers, fringe benefits can be expected to play a more important role in most organizations' personnel policies for the foreseeable future.

There are two keys to using fringe benefits policy entrepreneurially: knowing how to think about fringe benefits, and designing and maintaining a benefits policy that will complement the agency's unique human resource strategy. These two themes will meander in and out of what follows.

Health Insurance

We tend to think of health insurance as the Rock of Gibraltar of fringe benefits, but Princeton University's Uwe Reinhardt says that the concept of employer-provided health insurance is less than fifty years old, having been popularized during World War II as a way for clever employers to evade wage controls. Getting value to employees in the form of health insurance premiums evaded both the controls and taxation.

Today, health insurance is unequivocally the most important and expensive benefit employers typically provide. In a study I did a few years ago of nearly one hundred tax-exempt human service employers, health insurance took a full 70 percent of all dollars available for fringe benefits. In the past few years, health insurance costs for all employers have skyrocketed, and as of this writing there seems to be little relief in sight.

Who Owns?

If the fundamental causes for high health insurance premiums are beyond the individual agency, there are still several things the executive can do to help insure that his or her agency gets the best health benefits package available. The first is to answer a simple question: "Do you want to 'own' the health insurance group, or do you want someone else to 'own' it?" The way you answer this question sets the broad outlines of your agency's health insurance coverage.

The essence of "owning" your health insurance group is that employees' health choices, good and bad, have some sort of directly traceable impact on the rates their employer is charged. It can mean something as simple as arranging for a health insurance company such as Blue Cross/Blue Shield to treat the employer's employees as a group with its own unique set of benefits and its own schedule of premiums. Or it can mean setting up a full-blown self-insurance plan with a third party to administer a tailor-made package of benefits.

The advantages to "owning" your own health insurance group range from possible cost savings and tight management control to the opportunity to incorporate your own health care philosophy and even specific methods of treatment into your plan's design. The entrepreneurial instinct is always to own major projects like this, but a potentially major disadvantage is that it does put you squarely in the business of managing health care, and you need to ask yourself if that's really how you want to spend your time and your organization's.

Many nonprofit organizations choose to let others "own" the health insurance group serving their employees. This is what you're doing when you join a health maintenance organization (HMO) or a group composed of all employers in a designated geographic area. Both approaches typically use a method called community rating, in which all of the subscribers' experience is factored in before a rate is set. Since the numbers of people involved are so large, the fortunes (or misfortunes) of a single group of employees do not have much of an impact on the overall cost. Preferred provider organizations (PPO) function in much the same way, except that when a subscriber goes outside the group he or she must pay the difference between what the care would have cost with a preferred provider and what was actually charged.

Incidentally, until recently, the average employer had little say in how an HMO structured its rates. Recent federal legislation, however, has set the stage for HMOs to offer slightly different rates to certain groups within their membership based on actual experience—a kind of modified community rating approach. Nonprofits large enough to take advantage of the new rating may save some money if their HMO-using employees demonstrate a distinctly lower rate of use than the norm. Of course, the reverse could be true too.

Size Counts

In fringe benefits, especially in health insurance, size matters. Why? Insurance is essentially a device for coping with risk. Since the important question is not *whether* people will use their health insurance but *how much,* the major question becomes, Who bears the risk for unpredicted high usage? One way to make the risk acceptable is to make it predictable, and the best way to do that is to use the laws of probability. Once a group of employees gets large enough, the cost of its use of health care can be predicted with a fair amount of certainty from year to year.

It's that last phrase that is important. A group of fifty employees may have stable use, but one astronomical case will dramatically affect their costs whereas that same case in a group of five thousand will have far less catastrophic effects. Much of the administrative benefit to be derived from greater size rests on this simple principle. Associations can be helpful in this regard. See the appendix for a list of associations of nonprofits offering their members health insurance programs.

Some organizations have taken the principle one step further and put together what are called self-insured health insurance groups. These are either based in a single agency or draw employees from a number of cooperating agencies. There are two problems with self-insurance. One is that it is exceedingly difficult to put together enough nonprofit employees into a single group large enough to get the laws of probability working for you rather than against you. The other problem is that success in doing so only insures that the risk will be spread successfully, not that the underlying health care costs will be managed. For this reason and others, tax-exempt agencies, like most small businesses, are fast becoming HMO-dominated.

But if the locus of control of health insurance costs is beyond the reach of most nonprofit executives, shaping employees' decisions regarding their health insurance coverage is very much within it.

For the foreseeable future, health insurance costs will continue climbing, and even entrepreneurial nonprofit executives are going to need some help in coping. Nationally, health care inflation alone has been averaging in the mid to high single digits, and health insurance coverage itself has been increasing two to four times that fast. If your employees are not now contributing anything to their health insurance cost, ask them to start. This may sound like a page from the *Scrooge Handbook of Employee Relations,* but there's no better way to help them understand your struggle to contain health care costs or to begin preparing them to accept major changes in plan design, which you may need to consider down the road.

The larger opportunity here is to use personnel policies to sculpt the agency's work force. For example, two decades ago when large numbers of baby boomers flocked to public service, it was typical for the average nonprofit employer to offer employees health coverage only for individuals or the identical amount toward a family plan. As long as there was a never-ending supply of labor, and as long as that labor stayed single and childless and turned over quickly, the strategy worked.

In the late 1970s and 1980s, however, the situation changed. For one thing, the cost of health insurance began to increase disproportionately. Agencies responded by cutting back on the amount they paid. This strategy discouraged boomers building a family from staying, thereby prompting their nonprofit employers to try to hire more single, childless types just entering the work force— precisely the wrong labor market to woo, since by this time there were fewer of them and since other service-providing sectors of the economy needed a greater share. The opportunity for a limited number of agencies here would have been to deliberately target aging boomers with a nicely balanced package of salary and family-oriented benefits, paying for it with the savings that reduced turnover brings.

For the 1990s, demographers tell us that the single largest groups of new entrants into the work force will be women and immigrants. Also, we can expect to see the first wave of baby boomer retirees from large corporations and the military, who may well have at least partial health insurance benefits from their former careers. The entrepreneurial nonprofit executive will design an employee health insurance system with his or her agency's unique mix of labor markets in mind.

Life Insurance

Like the garlic bread in an Italian restaurant, life insurance tends to be noticed more for what accompanies it than for any exclusive properties it may possess. Organizations rarely purchase life insurance independent of every other coverage, and broad economic trends suggest that this connection will grow stronger in the future.

Employer-purchased life insurance is usually term insurance, meaning that the premium goes entirely toward the cost of the insurance for some predetermined term (such as the length of employment) with no built-up savings available to the employer/subscriber. It should cost pennies per day.

In concept, insuring lives is a rather simple matter. The insurance company collects premiums from a great many customers, keeps track of who paid it, and every now and then pays a claim. Problem is, the life insurance business isn't what it used to be, so many companies have begun diversifying into other types of personal insurance coverage such as health insurance. This is why employers often find life insurance programs linked with some other type of employee benefit. In fact, some experts suggest that traditional life insurance-oriented companies develop health and other types of coverages largely to lock in the relatively more lucrative life insurance business.

Life insurance coverages merit little routine attention beyond yearly reviews unless and until the nature of the employee population changes. With proper safeguards for confidentiality, they can tell a large employer or sponsoring association a great deal about the people they are hiring today versus those they hired a few years ago. In a large group, the incidence and nature of life insurance claims is one of the best ways to confirm a rise or fall in the overall quality of the work force. The mortality rates of higher paid and more educated personnel will typically be lower than those drifting in and out of lower-paying entry-level nonprofit jobs. As a direct consequence, the cost of life insurance will be less. Spotting trends like these early enough can shape hiring practices and help minimize the resultant costs of benefits.

Dental Insurance

Dental insurance is fast becoming a popular item for nonprofits that want to offer an extra benefit to employees. It's useful, relatively affordable, and easier to understand than most employee benefits. But there is a pitfall that employers must know about in order to maintain a successful dental insurance program.

Even the most expensive dental work is far less costly than the most expensive types of other medical procedures, so dental insurance premiums and claims payments can be projected much more precisely. The result for you, the employer, is that plan design and numbers of participants are the keys to making your dental insurance plan work well.

If you choose to run your own dental group, expect to pay for a substantial portion of your employees' premiums. Otherwise, employees with good dental health will opt out, while those with immediate needs will sign up quickly. It doesn't take an actuary to see that a group with that type of use won't survive. If you join someone else's group, chances are that group will also require minimum levels of employee participation and employer contribution for the same reason.

Retirement Benefits

The entrepreneurial nonprofit executive knows that success comes from an employee team that works well together and stays together. Many factors go into holding a group of employees together over time, but in the arena of benefits the glue is the agency's treatment of retirement. Moreover, as the population as a whole ages during the coming decades, individuals' plans for their old age will become a focal point in their employment choices. Farsighted executives instinctively know how to take advantage of their employees' upcoming shift in focus: beat them to it.

To get some idea of employers' choices in designing retirement plans, go down to the financial district of any major city on a nice day. Stand on a corner of your choosing and say ten times, in a loud voice, "I want to buy a retirement plan for my two hundred fifty employees." Your next problem will be crowd control.

Your second biggest problem will be sorting through a confusing array of retirement plan options. You can simplify things by asking yourself this question: "As an employer, do I want to specify the benefit that my employees receive upon retirement [defined benefit], or do I want to specify the amount that I contribute to the retirement plan each period [defined contribution]?"

For many nonprofit employers, to ask the question is to answer it. My research has shown that only about a third of nonprofit employees have access to a retirement option, and defined benefit plans require so much sophisticated actuarial analysis, complicated accounting, and involved reporting that few agencies can afford to offer them at all. Defined contribution plans have the advantage of easier administration and more controllable employer contributions. Little wonder that many employers in all fields are favoring defined contribution plans.

Incidentally, make a note to yourself for a few years from now. With the major emphasis on defined contribution plans, the risk of postretirement income shortfalls is borne almost exclusively by the retired person. For this and other reasons, today's idea of retirement will become a quaint relic within about twenty-five years. Instead, retirees will take part-time jobs more routinely and do other things to blur the distinction between active employment and jobless retirement (it's happening already, but the shift is likely to speed up soon). As that occurs, the flexible employer can tap into a rich part-time or second-career job market.

For now, take care to design your retirement plan so as to encourage employees to make a long-term commitment. Two areas that will help you do this are provisions for vesting and portability. Recent changes in federal law have limited the maximum period employees must wait before being vested in a retirement program (i.e., have the right to withdraw money), but a somewhat extended schedule is still possible. And choosing a plan that is not easily portable—meaning that it cannot easily be transferred if an employee resigns—will also encourage employees to remain with the organization.

In establishing a new retirement plan or reorganizing an old one, make yourself temporarily immune to the numbers the plan administrator promises. The best retirement plan is one which complements your organization's mission and is compatible with employee needs. An extra percent of future income or a degree more or less of risk should be a secondary choice made after assessing the plan's fit with agency mission and structure.

Open Your Own Cafeteria

One way to structure your benefit program so as to create maximum opportunity for employees is through a cafeteria plan (Section 125 plans, for you IRS code junkies). The principle behind a cafeteria plan is simple: each employee gets access to a certain amount of benefits of his or her own choosing or the equivalent in cash or some combination of the two. Designing and administering such a plan gets a bit complex, but it's worth it.

The inescapable problem with cafeteria plans is that they run counter to the time-honored way most small businesses, including nonprofits, afford fringe benefits: offer the benefits and hope no one takes them. Instead of paying only for the limited benefits that a limited number of employees choose, cafeteria plans essentially guarantee some sort of expenditure on behalf of every eligible employee. This means a dramatic bump up in overall benefit costs the first year the plan goes into effect.

Of course, once over that first hump, a cafeteria plan is a major attraction for employees and can be a cornerstone of recruitment, especially in an area where there are a number of similar agencies and none has a cafeteria plan. If you can possibly afford it, it's worth doing.

On the low end of the Section 125 continuum are pretax health and dependent care spending accounts, sometimes called salary reduction options. These plans, drawn from the same IRS code section as the one governing cafeteria plans, can mean a big win for everyone except the government since they allow employees to pay their share of benefit costs with before-tax dollars.

For example, if an employee making twenty-five thousand dollars yearly must pay a thousand dollars toward health insurance premiums, he or she must take that thousand dollars after it has passed through the tax screen. With a pretax spending account, the employee agrees to a voluntary reduction in salary of a thousand dollars. That money is then set aside, untaxed, for the exclusive purpose of paying for health insurance premiums. Neither the employee nor the employer pays taxes on that thousand dollars, so it ends up being the equivalent of, say, $1,250 or more on a taxable basis. Salary reduction plans can be used for health or dependent care expenses.

Naturally, there are problems with cafeteria plans. For the employer there is a certain fixed cost to establish one and to maintain the necessary filings with the IRS. Since the employee can get access to a yearly benefit at any time during the year, employers must necessarily gamble that the bulk of their employees will be sticking around (dependent care account spending is capped by law at five thousand dollars, and some employers are imposing health care account caps of two thousand dollars or so to minimize this problem). And the employee who sets aside some money for a year's worth of expenses and then for some reason doesn't use it for the intended purpose—loses it. Nevertheless, it's hard to imagine why employers of consequence *wouldn't* use at least a salary reduction plan for employees. P.S.: a good time to start is the same day an astronomical health insurance premium increase takes effect. Go ahead—look like a hero!

Back to the Future With Time

A final word on the traditional benefit offered up by nonprofit and other organizations when monetary compensation can't compete: time. The prospect of employees routinely receiving extra personal time is perhaps at the heart of what some mean when they speak of nonprofit "benefits." There are more than a few opportunities in managing employees' time allowances, as long as it is done with the greatest intelligence.

The entrepreneurial way to use time off is officially, formally, and with the organization's full support and encouragement. Surreptitiously allowing what should be a nine to five day to become ten to four may help equalize the per hour compensation package with for-profit equivalents, but the cost in eroded morale and a sloppy work ethic is too high. The alternative is to demand full performance when employees are on the job but build in generous time-off allowances.

One major nonprofit substance abuse services employer I know offers extraordinarily generous vacation time, starting new employees with four weeks off and rewarding veteran employees with as much as eight or ten weeks' vacation. The policy allows lower-paid employees to make extra money in temporary employment while still having enough time for a vacation. Professional employees, on the other hand, tend to spend at least some of the time pursuing professional interests. I know of a hospital chief financial officer who takes a month off every year to hike some far-flung mountain range—and invariably finds himself looking in on the local health care system. In these cases the agency benefits because many of its senior staff bring back a broadened perspective to what might otherwise become a very repetitive job.

There are some other ways to use time creatively. Job sharing and flex time are two ideas that should be more popular than they are in the corporate world, and they undoubtedly will be more popular as people familiar with the need for them move into corporate leadership roles. In the meantime, nonprofits that must compete with corporate employers can gain a few years' advantage by instituting these policies now. Chances are such a move would also mean a recruiting advantage over comparable nonprofit employers in the area.

Earned time is another time management device. Often employed by hospitals, earned time programs simply lump all holidays, vacation, and sick time allowances into a single yearly number of hours. Employees then earn one-twelfth of the yearly amount each month and can claim the paid time off simply by taking it. It tends to cut down on last-minute illnesses and "mental health days," thereby minimizing replacement costs and staff upheaval. The record keeping and possible contract renegotiations involved may be worth it.

More so than at any time in the past, benefits will be one of the most important job elements for tomorrow's nonprofit employees. Nonprofit organizations can no longer afford to assume that they are superior to other employers in this area. Some of the major strategies for improving employee benefits cost money, but the most powerful impact on benefits management comes from managers with a solid understanding of how their particular benefits package can support the right kind of work force.

CHAPTER 4

MYTH #4: WE CAN ALWAYS GET A GRANT

Looking for a chapter on how to write a concise problem state-ment, outline your proposed project's methods, devise a simple budget, and construct a program evaluation method?

Then stop right here. Go to your local library and take out some books on the subject. Mary Hall's *Getting Funded: A Com-plete Guide to Proposal Writing*[1] is a good publication, and *The Proposal Writer's Swipe File: 15 Winning Fund-Raising Proposals*[2] is a nice source. In any event, there are plenty of good guides to be found, and even a seasoned proposal writer will learn a great deal. But if that's what you're interested in, don't bother reading the rest of this chapter, because this is a chapter on how not to write a foundation proposal. To be more accurate, this is a chapter on *why* not to write a foundation proposal.

Who Gave?

College art students learn a concept called negative space. It's a simple but powerful idea. If you were to draw, say, that lamp next to you, one way to do it would be to carefully sketch every last detail of the lamp so that the average observer would recognize a lamp on your sketch pad. As an alternative, you could draw absolutely everything *except* the lamp, and observers would still recognize your picture as a lamp. This is what is known in art terms as negative space. It is also a pretty fair metaphor for grant

35

seeking in some nonprofit agencies: put down all of your projected expenses, compare them with projected revenues, and whatever amount is short is negative space—i.e., a grant.

The AFHV Model

To make some sense of the world of philanthropy, start with the 1990 television hit, "America's Funniest Home Videos."

No, I'm not joking. Be patient, it'll relate.

Go back to the first thirty years or so of popular television comedies. In both form and content, they were necessarily the product of a small circle of entertainment specialists, from stars to technical staffers. The shows were carefully scripted according to a quite rigid code of acceptable behavior (Rob and Laura Petrie on "The Dick Van Dyke Show" were married with a child, yet they always slept in twin beds five feet apart), and the story lines followed well-established patterns. Even the so-called spontaneous comedy show of the 1960s, "Candid Camera," was actually a collection of carefully staged events in which the only uncertainty was a single unsuspecting individual's reaction.

Call this the indirect approach to entertainment. For an opportunity to laugh, the country turned to a relatively small circle of priests and priestesses who carried out their mission along fairly well-determined lines. In effect, there was a three-way relationship among the viewer, the network which carried the program, and the people who produced it. For the viewer to be part of the production circle—and, therefore, to have some control over it— was completely out of the question.

Along came the home video camera in the 1980s, and suddenly the technology to produce good quality video work was within reach of the average person. The genius—and the source of intrigue—of "America's Funniest Home Videos" is that although the technology and other things like the genial banter of the host are still tightly controlled by the producers, the bulk of the content is not, leading to the unmistakable message that *this could be you.* Or someone you know. Or someone from the next town. In short, these are *real people.*

Now apply that same framework to philanthropy. In philanthropy the overwhelming majority of donations come from people needing a means of asset transfer no more complicated than cash or a checkbook. Grant guidelines, selection committees, proposal review systems—forget them all. Like "America's Funniest Home Videos," Americans as donors take matters of philanthropy into their own hands. Like "America's Funniest Home Videos" and its viewers, most philanthropy is a direct relationship between donor and recipient.

Where The Money Is

The statistics bear this out. Individuals are where the wealth is. One percent of the population controls nearly 30 percent of the wealth, a total of $4.3 trillion, or an amount slightly greater than the entire country's gross national product. Individuals are also where the donations come from. In 1987, according to the Independent Sector, a national association of nonprofits and foundations, 71 percent of all households reported donating to charity, and of those nearly 50 percent gave more than 1 percent of their yearly household income. Incredibly, 60 percent of the households who reported contributing had total incomes of less than $30,000, yet together this group gave nearly half of the total household contributions. Were giving money a matter for specialists, the patterns of giving would be far less widespread and concentrated in fewer hands.

Furthermore, the rate of increase in individuals' giving is second only to corporate giving (which, as we will see later, is very similar to individual giving) in its average yearly rate of increase during the last two decades.

Average Yearly Rate of Increase
1970–1988

Corporations	Individuals	Bequests	Foundations
10.42	9.77	6.7	6.7

Even more revealing, individuals' share of total national contributions has increased significantly, while foundation giving has fallen:

Contribution Sources as Percent of Total
1970–1988

	Corporations	Foundations	Bequests	Individuals
1970	4	9	10	77
1988	5	6	7	82

What's happening here? Is there some revolution going on in the philanthropic world to which nonprofit managers are not privy? The answer is almost certainly no, that individuals have always been the source of most giving, and that entrepreneurial nonprofit managers have known this fact right along. Donors like the one-to-one contact that can come with a charitable contribution, and patterns of giving reflect that fact. It is no accident that direct mail technology improved markedly during the '70s and '80s—for example, 26 percent of those donating to environmental charities in 1987 did so because they received a letter—nor is it merely by chance that the art of fund raising has seen such steady expansion and acceptance as a distinct profession.

The New Corporate Approach

What's more, there is evidence to suggest that the insistence on the personal touch will continue in ways that are only now beginning to become clear. Take corporate philanthropy programs, for example. Corporate giving was the fastest growing type of philanthropy during the past two decades, and although its annual growth rate has leveled off in recent years, its donations carry disproportionate weight because corporations have begun to learn how to combine large gifts with a specific focus.

Ben and Jerry's Ice Cream has one of the best examples of extraordinarily committed and targeted philanthropy, but there are hundreds of others. I know of one large pharmacy chain that for years had had a nicely enlightened policy of allowing each local store to contribute a certain amount of its pretax profits to the charity of its choice. The result was an uninspired hodgepodge of charitable gifts. Satisfied with the policy but unhappy with the ineffectiveness of the implementation, the company started examining alternatives. In the process, it began asking itself what type of customer it wanted in its stores. The profiles varied widely according to the location of each store, but the theme that quickly emerged was that the best customers were the elderly who lived nearby.

Further, the major threats to the stores' retaining an elderly customer were death and a nursing home. Presumably the pharmacy was already doing its part to handle the first problem, but the company realized that the second was a double threat. Not only did nursing homes take away a good customer, but they might very well transfer that customer to one of the hated mail-order pharmacy houses. That settled it. Today, the pharmacy chain has a company-wide policy encouraging local store managers to donate an even larger share of pretax profits to local nonprofit home health care organizations.

A similar kind of thing is happening in the foundation world, particularly community fund-raising efforts like the United Way. In years past, donors simply handed over their money to the fund-raising group, which then set about to distribute it according to its own assessment of need and worthiness. Today, that practice is diminishing as donors' choices are incorporated into more community-wide fund-raising campaigns. Donor choice has already been used in many cities for many years.

By lessening some of the influence of community fund staff and allocation volunteers, donor choice follows the "America's Funniest Home Videos" path to more direct communication between source and user.

It also presents distinct headaches for grant recipients, whose yearly income can rise or fall on the strength of their name recognition and reputation. Since it can be argued that the average business's fortune rises or falls on the strength of the same things, it's a little hard for nonprofit managers to cry discrimination. In the long run that won't work anyway, so the only choice is to make sure that one's agency is well positioned and thoroughly recognized in the minds of the donors.

Who Got?

Where all this leads is a fair question at this point. What, in other words, can the entrepreneurial nonprofit manager learn from this myth-busting? To answer that question, we must now match our original question "who gave?" with another one: "who received?"

At $48 billion of a total $105 billion donated, religious groups accounted for 46 percent. Combine this fact with the percentage of giving done by individuals, and we can say that for every dollar donated by an individual to some tax-exempt recipient in this country, there is a 38 percent chance that it will go to some sort of religious-affiliated group.

Many nonreligious nonprofit managers sigh in resignation, certain that such concentrated success in fund raising is the sole province of religious organizations. That may be understandable, but it's not productive. Instead, the entrepreneurial nonprofit manager asks what he or she can take away from such obvious success.

A lot, as it turns out. But before we start, I should say in all seriousness that the following analysis is deliberately narrowly focused and intends no disrespect for organized religion in general or any religion in particular. There are many things about religion that transcend mere analysis, and many things that cannot possibly be included in such an abbreviated exploration as this one. In short, because the whole story is so large, we must concentrate on only a small part of it.

Why Religious Giving Is So Powerful

For an insight into how religious groups motivate philanthropy, listen to the language of religions when describing those associated with it. They are *members* of a *congregation* or *temple* or *parish*. They are *communicants, children of God, brothers* and *sisters*. They often must symbolically enter a *house* of worship. Many religions stress *brotherhood* and talk about the family of humankind. This is the language of inclusion and exchange, and the overall effect is to create a sustained sense of belonging, a long-term membership in an entity larger than oneself.

What else does the religious affiliation offer? A part of personal identity, for one thing. It means something to be a member of a church, one aspect of which is that a great deal of the preliminary work of introduction and familiarization can be presumed to have been done when one member asks another for a donation. Religious membership fulfills spiritual needs, obviously, but interestingly enough a frequently cited reason for donating to religious nonprofits is a belief in the organization as a worthy cause that helps the poor and needy.

Frequent contact is another advantage the religious fund raiser can count. In 1988, two-thirds of all Americans reported belonging to a church or synagogue, and of that number two-thirds reported attending that church or synagogue at least once during a typical week. Perhaps most important, religious affiliation can touch that part of us seeking deeper meaning and a reason to hope, intangibles more powerful than measurable.

Add it all up. Inclusion and communication, personal identity, helping others, constant contact, connection with our deeper selves: in the scale of what's good and noble about human beings, everything else is chopped liver. Looked at this way, is it any wonder that religious organizations top all other forms of tax-exempt entities in dollars donated?

The Entrepreneurial Opportunity

Now turn it around. Apply the same standards to nonreligious tax-exempt organizations, and you will see a distinct pattern emerge: *the elements that lead to successful fund raising in the religious sector are virtually identical to those that succeed in nonreligious fund raising.*

Let's apply that notion to the four sources of philanthropic contributions to see what implications it has for the entrepreneurial nonprofit manager. For these purposes, our four categories are really only two: individual giving and bequests, and corporation and foundation giving.

Including large numbers of individuals in the work of your organization is a matter of attitude, not technology. The American Cancer Society and Habitat for Humanity are two brilliant examples of organizations that have mastered the art of including large numbers of people in the delivery of their mission. Although it might very well be possible to deliver the same service in a different manner, the inclusion of many people in such personal ways is both a means of getting the job done and an end in itself.

Part of involving large numbers of people in the organization's mission is communication, and part of communication is constant contact. I have always found the written word in the form of newsletters, memos, personal letters, and notes to be reliable means of maintaining contact with members (and that's really the status you are striving to achieve in the inclusion phase of your fund raising). But the written word needs to be backed up by personal contact.

Keeping this fact in mind for certain types of services is particularly important. When people who give to charities are asked why they did so, contributors to some of the less glamorous charities such as human services and youth development more often respond that they were personally asked to give rather than that they decided to give on their own.

The shrewd funds seeker knows that giving his or her recipients a sense of identity not only helps get today's donation, it helps seal tomorrow's too. Giving donors a sense of identity can mean just about anything from a wallet-sized membership card to a high visibility media push. But the real area to capitalize on here comes from a funny twist in the fund-raising business. Ask people who have actually donated to a given charity why they did so and you often hear something like they wanted "to give something back to the community." It's as if the nonprofit were in the foreground receiving the actual dollars, but in the background is the real target, "the community." In this sense the recipient agency becomes a kind of tangible representation of the abstract idea of a community. If your institutional ego can stand a secondary role, subtly evoking this connection in your approach can be quite powerful.

Incidentally, bequests for our purposes are really simply an extension of individual-based fund raising, but they represent one of the greatest areas of future potential for entrepreneurial gains in planned giving.[3] Demographer Harold Hodgkinson told *The Non-Profit Times* that the baby boomer/yuppie wave will be unprecedented in absolute earning power. Yet that same cohort is reproducing itself at something like an 85–90 percent rate, meaning that an unusually potent earning force with an unusually small number of offspring will be writing wills making an unusually large number of gifts to philanthropy.

Why You Can't Always Plan to Get a Grant

By now it is obvious why managing a nonprofit organization as though you can always get a grant is risky business. Yet to go in the other direction and rule out grants entirely would be a mistake for most organizations. The fact is that corporate and foundation grants are a legitimate and valuable revenue source for nonprofit organizations. The secret is to make sure the amount of grant money coming in exceeds the effort required to secure it.

Happily, the rules for marketing your agency to corporate and foundation givers are the same as for marketing to individual givers. Of course, the way those rules get played out is often different, so it pays to learn the nuances.

One of the best things you can do is to shake off any preconceptions you may have about the foundation world having networks of good ol' boys and girls who've known each other for a long time. *Of course it does.* But so do postal carriers, physicians, Subaru dealers, and professional violinists. The question is not whether foundation types form circles of professional friends and allies, but what you can do to become part of those circles. Here's a quick and easy way to start: invite one of them somewhere. Anywhere. For any reason. Except to ask them for a grant.

Some years ago in a terrific little essay titled, "While You're

Up, Get Me a Grant," William Lee Miller of the Poynter Center at Indiana University told this story:

> Once an associate and I had lunch with Joel Colton of the Rockefeller Foundation, at our request but his expense. Midway through the meal's cautious conversation Mr. Colton had an obviously liberating perception. "You mean you aren't going to ask for *anything?*" He said it with a touch of incredulity. His eyes lit up. He visibly relaxed. His face unwound into a smile. "Well, then. WELL, then. Let's have dessert!"

Foundation and corporation givers are like everyone else; they like to be included. Usually they are under no illusions about why they're being included, but inclusion is inclusion regardless of ulterior motives. An invitation to your annual meeting, a casual lunch, a spot on your mailing list—all of these are relatively easy ways to include foundation representatives. But to be most effective, you have to do this before, during, and after the times when you are seeking funds directly.

Would *You* Pay Fifty Thousand Dollars for a Piece of Paper?

Just as with individual donors, constant contact is supremely important, especially when you are not seeking money. (You're right, what I am suggesting *is* that you sell the agency, and if you don't believe enough in what you're doing to sell it, then step aside and let someone try who does). Again, contact can be personal, over the telephone or through the mail, and using all three is preferable. Inclusion and contact build the grantor's sense of identification with the agency and help establish confidence in its abilities. After all, a grant proposal is nothing more than a promise written on a piece of paper. As a funder, you would feel more comfortable knowing that today's promise was preceded by lots of kept promises, wouldn't you?

Marketing your program to foundation and corporate givers does differ from marketing it to individual donors in one or two profoundly different ways, however. For one thing, administration is often a terribly dirty word to those who fund and run foundations, and unlike the individual donor of $100, the grantor of $10,000 can more easily stipulate that every last dollar go to program services instead of winding up in the presumed black hole labeled "administration." This is unfortunate but can sometimes be avoided by a bit of judicious donor education.

The Innovation Treadmill

The more insidious effect is what I call the Innovation Treadmill. The majority of grants for operating expenses are limited to terms of one, three, or five years or the like. Ostensibly, the recipient uses the funding as seed money to start up a demonstrably worthwhile program, support for which materializes from just about any other source during the seed phase. Future years' grants that would have gone to the new service can then be directed to a completely different area of need.

This cycle has two primary effects, both of them undesirable. The best known of the two is that we recipients jump enthusiastically onto the treadmill, repackaging existing services so as to fit the funding fad of the year. In effect, we always get the same grant, it's just named differently and targeted to a slightly different area of need.

The second effect is much more subtly dangerous. Catching on to the repackaged grant routine—or just plain interested in another area of need altogether—givers take their largess elsewhere. Then, after a cycle of grants in that area, they move onto a third area and then a fourth. Each time they leave behind organizations or programs that can survive, but just barely. The overall effect is to create a weakened service delivery system, like a field planted with a hundred seedlings that may or may not make it till the harvest, instead of ten plants that definitely will.

No Bad Guys Here

Are grantors being shortsighted or self-indulgent when they follow this pattern? Absolutely not. In reality, it is actually a very rational response to an overwhelming fact of life. Publicly supported foundations, especially community foundations, by definition derive their support from public sources. In order to keep donors' attention, the fund raiser needs to motivate them. The easiest way to motivate givers is to give them a new reason to give, so the pressure is permanently on to come up with a new and even more compelling object of philanthropy every year.

Does all this mean that the entrepreneurial nonprofit manager cannot and should not attempt to get grants? Quite the contrary. Grants offer great flexibility and the opportunity for intensive community involvement to just about any nonprofit organization and should be sought for these reasons alone. But receipt of a grant is really the end of a lengthy marketing process, not the beginning, and because of this most organizations cannot depend on grants to fill the holes in budgets created by shortfalls in other revenues. The wise entrepreneurial nonprofit manager rules his or her grant program, not vice versa.

C H A P T E R   5

MYTH #5: IT'S BETTER IF IT'S DONATED

The insidiousness of this myth began to dawn on me one hot June afternoon. I had just driven onto a town's third street named Washington in search of a used 1979 Apple computer donation. We desperately needed a computer at my new agency, and a coworker had a friend who had a friend . . .

Nine-thirty-three Washington Street was not at all the kind of house where you would expect to find the respected CEO reported to be the ultimate owner of the machine. Its postage-stamp lawn was about two weeks beyond a good mowing, and the shrubs had yet to see a pair of shears that season. I parked the car and bounded up the flagstone walk, carefully avoiding the missing stones. As I landed on the tiny porch there was an explosion somewhere within the house (Woof).

I glanced inside the screen door. Inside on the left was a heavy-looking wood door, to the right a carpeted stairway. Across the hall was a hand-lettered banner saying "Welcome Home, Daddy," with something about Singapore in the lower right corner. A handful of unmatched balloons hung from the banner.

I pushed the door bell. No sound. I pushed it again. There was another explosion inside, this one softer and more tentative (Woof). Still no door bell sound. I knocked on the door and waited (Woof). Nothing stirred. I knocked again (Woof).

A teenager appeared at the top of the stairway and started down. He was about fifteen, with blond, shoulder-length hair and an "Aerosmith World Tour" T-shirt.

47

"Hi," I said, acutely conscious of my adulthood. In the distance, the explosions resumed. "Is Dick (Woof!) Campbell (Woof!) in (Woof!)?"

"What?'

"Dick (Woof!) Campbell (Woof!) in (Woof!)?"

"What?" He scowled and yelled over his shoulder "Ma! Keep her quiet!" Then he motioned me outside, closing the screen door and the outside door behind both of us. It was a practiced move.

I said, "Is Dick Campbell in?"

"No."

I remembered why I never wanted to teach high school. "Well, he was going to give us a computer."

"Oh. It's up here." He turned and reentered the house. I followed. We went up the stairs and turned into his room. Every available inch was covered with something. The centerpiece was a six-foot-high poster of Aerosmith on one wall. There were four huge speakers under and on top of what appeared to be a desk, and a bright red Fender guitar lay propped against an amplifier. "Right there," he said, pointing to the Apple computer sitting under a stack of Black Sabbath records and a layer of dust.

Gingerly, I removed the records and looked for the computer's power cords. I had never even seen a personal computer before, let alone transported one, so I worked carefully. When I turned to say I was ready, my host had disappeared. Shrugging to myself and emboldened by my mechanical success so far, I piled the components on top of each other. They looked heavy but the pile was surprisingly light, so I decided to take the whole thing in a single trip.

I was at the top of the stairs when I saw the limousine pull up in front of the house. It was big, black, and shiny, and a uniformed chauffeur was driving.

I was halfway down the stairs when I realized that the explosions had started up again (Woof), this time accompanied by footsteps. Three steps from the bottom, the explosions grew much louder (WOOF) and more frequent (WOOF, WOOF). Suddenly the heavy interior door flew open and a blond female blur shot out ("DADDY!"). Startled, I missed a step and pitched toward the remaining two. As I struggled to keep my balance, the explosions headed toward me (WOOF! WOOF! WOOF!).

I came to an awkward halt just shy of the now slamming screen door as a dog the size of a Shetland pony bounded out of the wooden door. It saw me and the shuddering screen door at the same time (WOOF! WOOF! WOOF!) and drew up short (WOOF!).

For a moment, it regarded me quizzically. That was all the time I needed. I pushed open the door and backed my way onto the porch.

Down at the limousine, the greeting continued. "DADDY! How was *Ireland*?" I looked up. On the porch with me was Aerosmith. He looked at me blankly. I grinned. "I thought it was Singapore," I said.

"What?"

"Never mind." At times like these one must be supremely self-confident. I drew myself up as straight as my load of computer components would allow and strode down the walk. Dick Campbell met me halfway, the blur now hanging on to his arm. "Oh, the computer," he said. "Enjoy it!" And then, as I was almost past him, he cheerfully called out, "Just have it back by September."

Our internal communication, it would turn out, had broken down. Yes, the computer was to be donated—but only for the summer. It was several days before I could even bring myself to look at the damn thing after I carted it to the office, and a few weeks before I had the heart to learn how to run it. As it happened, it wouldn't do what we wanted a computer to do anyway. That September, we did what we should have done in the first place—we went to a computer store and bought the software we needed and some hardware to run it.

Whence the Myth Comes

The "It's Better If It's Donated" myth is one of the most wasteful a nonprofit executive can believe. It endures because getting people to donate things can be great fun (sometimes), it produces a tangible outcome, and it's enormously self-justifying to boot. It's the unseen corollary to the something-for-nothing syndrome afflicting just about all novice nonprofit managers.

In-kind donations are a peculiar type of transaction and require a special kind of hustle. The most successful in-kind donations fund-raising consultant I ever met was a fellow who had once completed an all-expense paid vacation at Leavenworth Federal Prison, the result of a string of highly professional confidence games. What made him so good in our sector was that he hadn't let prison change his methods, he'd just learned how to point them in a different direction.

Textbook of Bad Economics

Why aren't in-kind donations a better source of leverage for the nonprofit executive? Because they're bad economics. Consider the economic life cycle of the average in-kind donation.

First, the owner acquires the product, presumably deliberately, because in some way it fulfills his/her/its need. What are the chances that a potential recipient has precisely the same set of specifications as the original owner? Slim. So any secondary user will almost certainly have to settle for less efficiency in the product's use than the original purchaser.

Next, the owner must decide that the product is no longer of value to him/her/it. This condition may come about because the product is too old, a new and better product has become available, or because a cheaper alternative has presented itself. In any case, the decision to part with it as a tax-exempt donation can only come after the acquisition/disposition decision. By the time the process reaches the receiving nonprofit, there have been lots of compromises made, and the probability is high that the product will prove unworkable in the end.

This is exactly the process that occurred in a school system I know of that received an impressive donation of computer hardware and software. The computer company was more than happy to make the donation for the public relations value as well as the tax write-off, and the school was more than happy to accept.

Until they tried to use the system. The computer company made the donation in the first place because that particular line was being replaced with an updated version. There was nothing wrong with the computers themselves, they were just superceded by more powerful new models.

The problem was that the computers didn't do what the school system needed them to do, *and* they needed large amounts of training and other support that the schools weren't prepared to acquire. The system ended up unused. A worse fate is perhaps that the donation gets used but is so hobbled by trade-offs that it is functionally impaired. Managerially, this is a regressive process, and it accounts for some of the self-imposed technological backwardness characteristic of some nonprofits.

How to Make It Work (If You Can't Help Yourself)

The underlying problem with most in-kind donations is their hit-or-miss nature. If the overall volume of both donations and recipients could be greatly expanded and the frequency made more regular, many of the advantages to both sides could be cemented. This is the principle behind NAEIR (National Association for the Exchange of Industrial Resources), a kind of national broker of donated goods. Major corporations get the tax advantage of donations, while nonprofits self-select themselves. Together, they can make the most efficient use of the property no longer wanted by original purchasers. That's an entrepreneurial twist to an old problem, and it may be one your agency can duplicate—but only if it's willing to devote staff time and resources to the job, much as one would to a more traditional development effort.

The next time you feel tempted to run after a donated item, do a simple calculation. Estimate its value as of the time you would expect to acquire it. Then, calculate the number of hours it will take you to secure it. Multiply that number by your hourly salary. Increase it by whatever percentage of salary you receive in fringe benefits. Increase this number by 50 percent to account for the overhead that you will use up in the chase. Now compare the two numbers. If the item's value is well above the total cost of your time—and if you can think of no more profitable way to spend the time—start the chase. Otherwise, think again.

There are, of course, exceptions to the rule of donations' costliness, and volume is usually at the core of them. Many food programs, for example, have devised ingenious food recycling efforts involving businesses. In some ways, traditional food co-ops capitalize on donated labor to make the difference between low prices and market pricing for members. Then there is also the matter of donated capital goods.

Donated capital goods, particularly buildings and other high-cost fixed assets, are almost always worthwhile. An asset of that caliber is virtually always worth getting donated, even if it means endless hours of effort by the chief executive or other top manager. Given recent tax reforms, it's also a fairly unlikely happening.

Another circumstance in which donated goods have a role is when it is in the recipient nonprofit's interest to make the donor feel appreciated via the donation. I used to have a board member of my small nonprofit agency serving mentally retarded adults who routinely proffered her husband's old business suits to the clients. What she failed to see was that clothing that fit her football player-sized husband was useless for small, mentally retarded men, especially when the suits were a bit threadbare in the first place. Still, it was her way of being helpful, so the only proper course of action was to smile, say thank you, and look for the nearest dumpster.

Yet another situation in which nonprofits have to pursue donated goods is the various governmental programs of the '70s and '80s requiring new in-kind matches. Less popular now, the major attribute of these types of governmental funding is that they at least make explicit the government's determination not to pay full price.

It's not always better if it's donated. Securing donated goods eats up resources that would otherwise go to operations. Unless the process is expanded and incorporated into your organization's routine, or unless the donations are capital goods, the donated goods chase is a time waster. Entrepreneurial executives avoid it whenever they can.

CHAPTER 6

MYTH #6: WE DON'T PAY OUR BILLS ON TIME

Just because it's a myth doesn't mean it's wrong. Often, nonprofit organizations do *not* pay their bills on time, for a few very good reasons which we will go into later. But if the problem is real, the hoopla created around it by the people owed the money is a bit suspect.

Stretching Exercises

Yes, slow payments from their nonprofit customers are a real problem for many suppliers of goods and services. But slow payments in general are a problem for every type of business, especially services, because once the service is delivered it can't be revoked, and the supplier is essentially at the mercy of the purchaser. Many service businesses report lengthening collection periods for just this reason.

The reputation for slow payment to their suppliers by nonprofits is magnified because so much of what nonmedical nonprofit corporations purchase, outside of personnel and occupancy expenses, is from service providers and therefore is easier to ignore. It also happens to be intimately related to the financial structure of nonprofit organizations themselves.

To put it simply, nonprofit corporations have a limited number of places where they can get capital. Whereas for-profit groups can attract investors in myriad ways, the only "investors" that

53

tax-exempt organizations can get are those willing to part with their money completely. Because of this situation, nonprofit executives must look for other sources of money, and inevitably the easiest and cheapest source is right under their pens: unpaid bills.

For a more detailed explanation of how nonprofit organizations satisfy their need for capital see Chapter 9, To Own or Not to Own, and Other Silly Questions. For now, understand that the carefully selected unpaid bill is an essential item in the average nonprofit executive's financial toolbox. In fact, it is in the executive's interest to stretch every payable right up to its limit, and the entrepreneurial nonprofit executive will do just that.

How do you know when you've reached the limit? When a payable costs more than one dime in interest or penalties (the difference is semantic). When the supplier threatens to cut off further shipments or demands cash up-front before the next transaction. When an influential supplier is heard grumbling about your payment policies. In short, when the cost of not paying exceeds the cost of paying (and the word cost here means more than simply monetary cost).

The only way to milk your payables is to do it vendor by vendor. Establish a sensible minimum yearly purchase level and focus only on vendors from whom you routinely purchase more than that amount. Determine an acceptable payment period and stick to it, but be flexible enough to change it—perhaps permanently—when circumstances change. Above all, keep on top of the system every day. Drawing out the payment period unfortunately reduces the number of days in which you can correct unforeseen problems, so stay on top of it.

Ironically, your vendors will probably cooperate fully with your plans. Not happily, but fully. The idea that nonprofit organizations are slow in paying their bills is so indelibly stamped on most people in business that they expect it from you. Use it, even if you don't need it. I have seen transactions where a business let a nonprofit customer avoid paying for much longer periods than it would have allowed another proprietary interest. There's a term for this practice from the nonprofit's perspective: *free money*.

It's Not Slow Payment They're Worried About

Lest you think that the preceding is formal advice to stiff your vendors, let me add that the handling of bills owed is one area where traditional nonprofit management thinking diverges from the for-profit business approach. A thousand-dollar invoice seems to the recipient tax-exempt agency to be formal notification of a binding legal and moral responsibility to pay the thousand dollars. To the vendor who sent it, it is more like a fond hope.

The reason for this difference lies in different business cultures. Nonprofits' behavior as customers is different because their behavior as suppliers is different.

Take the question of permanently unpaid bills, for instance. To tax-exempt organizations who get no revenue from individuals, the prospect of a permanently unpaid bill or bad debt is usually a foreign experience. Yet for the average proprietary business it's a fact of life, accounting for as much as 1 or 2 percent of revenue each year. Don't let them mislead you: it's not slow pay they're worried about, it's *no pay*.

Fortunately, as slow as some nonprofit groups can be about paying their bills, my experience suggests that there are few deadbeats among them. Partly this comes from the cultural expectations described above, but it is also partly due to the high level of government funding most nonprofit corporations receive today. If the government is good for the money, its nonprofit recipient will be too.

Nonprofits also tend to be hesitant about pushing vendors because many need not worry about realization percentages or where they set their prices. The concept of realization is particularly foreign to most nonprofit organizations. When a business, especially a professional service, delivers something worth a thousand dollars according to its standards and gets paid a thousand dollars, its realization is 100 percent. But when that same business gets paid a thousand dollars for a service that should have cost fifteen hundred dollars according to its standard way of pricing its services, then its yield is 67 percent, or:

$$\$1,000 \div \$1,500.$$

The second scenario could have happened in any number of ways. For example, the business could have agreed ahead of time to limit itself to a top billing of a thousand dollars. Or it could have agreed not to bill for certain costs of providing the service. Or it could have billed fifteen hundred dollars and received a thousand dollars before the customer went bankrupt. Whatever the reason, the company judges its success in the transaction according to how close its realization percentage came to its desired overall percentage. Retail stores operate the same way, except that their realization overall gets reduced by all of the above factors plus the effects of special sales, discounts, and pilferage.

The underlying aspect of managing realization is that the company will price so as to support its desired level of return, and that that price, if possible, will take into account all of the things that can happen to reduce profit. By contrast, most nonprofit corporations do little pricing, if only because revenue tends to come in predetermined amounts from major funding sources. Budgeting in this setting then means backing into the revenue available.

In effect then, nonprofit entities take their knockdowns and make their compromises, before even entering into a transaction. Consequently, it rarely occurs to them in their role as purchasers that their vendors might actually be expecting to give discounts, put up with late payments, suffer bad debts, etc.—if not from them, then at least from some portion of their customers. When it comes to discounts and no-cost slow payments, why not oblige?

Stretching your payables should come from careful planning and shrewd insight into your vendors, not from a fumbled cash flow. Current bills owed are one of the nonprofit's few sources of relatively inexpensive capital. Stringing them out should be done systematically and monitored constantly. When it is, the entrepreneurial nonprofit executive performs the ultimate coup: turning a liability into an asset.

CHAPTER 7

MYTH #7: NONPROFIT EXECUTIVES ARE LOUSY MANAGERS

With the possible exception of sex and personal income, few subjects are more likely to make the average professional adult self-conscious than a discussion of his or her management skills. Management has become the secular religion of the twentieth century, its practitioners the high priests and priestesses. Individual performances are forever being compared to some unarticulated standard and usually found wanting. The loser then skulks away, determined to redeem a small measure of self-esteem by initiating a similar discussion with someone sure to be found even more inadequate.

Typically this particular buck stops with nonprofit organizations. Manager bashing in this field is second nature for the vast majority of the public—and many nonprofit executives as well. Why? Let's take a look at what this myth is all about, how it gets its nourishment, and what the practicing nonprofit executive can do about it.

Characteristics of Leadership

James Kouzes of the Tom Peters Group and Harry Posner of Santa Clara University's Leavy School of Business Administration teamed up recently to study the characteristics most people admire and look for in a leader.[1] Here they are:

1. Honest
2. Competent
3. Forward-looking
4. Inspiring
5. Intelligent
6. Fair-minded
7. Broad-minded
8. Courageous
9. Straightforward
10. Imaginative
11. Dependable
12. Supportive
13. Caring
14. Cooperative
15. Mature
16. Ambitious
17. Determined
18. Self-controlled
19. Loyal
20. Independent

Kouzes and Posner say that the first four characteristics—honest, competent, forward-looking, and inspiring—were the four regularly selected as most important in every setting they examined.

Now, assuming that this list is a decent representation of what it takes to be a leader in any field, ask yourself this question: *Is it logical that one type of organization would have many leaders and another type of organization none at all, solely on the basis of their respective tax statuses?* The answer to the question is self-evident. So how come nonprofit organizations are often perceived to be poorly managed? The answer is complex and a bit speculative, but working it through will suggest ways for the entrepreneurial nonprofit manager to begin correcting this imbalance both for himself or herself and for the field.

Size Matters

One of the reasons why nonprofit corporate leaders are rarely included in the company of respected managers, limited though that temple may be, is that in order to make a national manage-ment hero there needs to be a national base to manage. Because most nonprofits are small and more or less regionally oriented, their managers fail this test right away. Further, most national management heroes got that way either by working their way up through a large national or multinational company, or by taking a small one and making it national. For the latter managers, it is typically the act of making very small become very large that brings them recognition, the underlying message being that growth alone signifies good management ability.

In this respect, nonprofit organizations are really little different from the average small business. Both types of managers toil in obscurity and will continue to unless discovered by a reporter or business philosopher. Especially in the case of the for-profit that has grown explosively, the celebrity comes after the fact and tends to be analytical rather than predictive. The major difference is that most nonprofit managers simply do not have the opportunity to build a nationally oriented corporation.

Another size-related reason why nonprofit managers rarely get the recognition accorded their for-profit counterparts is a bit more subtle. If one analyzes the business world's compensation prac-tices, it might appear that compensation decisions generally are made on the basis of levels of responsibility. But in reality the broad patterns suggest that managerial compensation is more often determined *according to the incumbent's routine proximity to decisions about the use of capital*. The closer a manager is expected to be to decisions about investments, purchases, mergers, borrow-ing, etc., the higher his or her salary is likely to be. Not an inviolate rule, of course, but it will suffice for a general pattern.

When those who would judge managerial performance accept this unarticulated value, nonprofit managers lose out in two ways. First, as we will see later on, nonprofits as a class are extremely undercapitalized. And second, because nonprofits rightfully see the accumulation of capital as a tool in the service of mission rather than an end in itself, the attention of the judges tends to get diverted to those organizations who put the accumulation of capital higher on the list.

Crossing the Gulf of Lingo

To be fair, it works in the other direction too. Over the years, many nonprofits have carefully and deliberately rejected the standards of measurement with which traditional business lives. This is particularly clear when it comes to the terminology of business. We have created a Gulf of Lingo between us and the rest of the business world, perhaps without realizing it. We call marketing "development," we call net worth "fund balance," and we'd rather not call profit anything at all. Consequently, even the most rudimentary communication between business and nonprofits is subject to mistranslation and misunderstanding.

But perhaps the most fundamental reason why nonprofit managers get overlooked in assessments of management skill is that we often don't even know there's a contest going on. Ironically, the same passion and commitment to mission that often brought the manager into the field is a disadvantage here. It tends to focus the organization's leadership attention inward, since it is in the daily workings of the entity that the evolution of the mission can be seen most clearly.

The problem with an inward focus of leadership roles is that it confuses internal responsibilities and leaves the major executive role untended.

In any organization, it is the role of executives to cope with change in the external environment, the role of managers to cope with complexity. When the person or persons at the top of the organization focus primarily on the admittedly compelling day-to-day details of making things work inside the organization, two negative things happen. The first is that the managers whose job it is to handle the complexities of changing grow confused and resentful of the interference, or else they develop the bad habits of indifference or overdependence that interference encourages.

In the long run, the second outcome is the more worrisome. By focusing what should be executive energies on the internal workings of the organization, the *non*entrepreneurial nonprofit executive deprives the organization of its most important natural pipeline to and from the outside world. I once asked the executive director of a mid-sized nonprofit corporation to participate on a panel discussion scheduled for six weeks later. She asked what date it was, and upon learning that it was the second Wednesday of the month she promptly declined. It turned out that every second and fourth Wednesday she had to do the agency's payroll. Now that's an attitude waiting to be blindsided by change.

Another reason why nonprofit managers get less than a fair share of recognition is the absence of an agreed-upon standard of effectiveness, otherwise known as the Bottom Line. While non-profits certainly do have a bottom line, in the sense of there being a point beyond which some sort of outside force refuses to let an organization continue, nonprofits' bottom line is a great deal closer to bottom than is for-profits'.

The more practical application of the bottom line standard is as a measurement of profitability. As flawed as this type of standard is, it at least gives insiders and outsiders alike a common point by which to judge actions. Nonprofit organizations do not have this luxury and never will. Since there is no agreed-upon and objectively measurable standard of outcome, the constant danger in a nonprofit organization is that evaluation of effort becomes intensely personal. With no quantifiable rallying point for those inside the organization, the personal tastes of whomever happens to be in power are the de facto standards for judging performance. This is why ordinary interpersonal political battles can get so openly ferocious in a nonprofit. Often no one has the moral authority to shut them off, and the warning of quantifiable harm to the organization is clearly empty.

The Things Nonprofits Do Right

Happily, there are a good many things that nonprofit organizations typically do exactly the right way. Even more happily, people are beginning to recognize them. Credit Peter Drucker for officially inaugurating public consciousness raising on this topic.

Nonprofit organizations, he says, are actually more sophisticated and effective than their for-profit counterparts in matters of organizational strategy.[2] He explains that this is true because the nonprofit organization starts with its mission and builds itself around it. The result is a focused organization with specific strategies for specific goals. Starting with the mission and then making administrative decisions creates discipline and a shared sense of focus that concentrates resources on a very small number of interrelated projects.

In a positive sense, money is secondary to most nonprofit strategy. First comes agreement on the area or areas of focus. By contrast, Drucker says, most for-profit businesses start (and sometimes end) their planning with financial returns. The result, as management gurus and op-ed pieces tell us frequently, is a business world run only by the numbers with no sense of itself and no ability to motivate beyond the next quarterly returns or biweekly paycheck. Paradoxically, the nonprofit approach often results in more revenue to the organization than if it had set out to accomplish only that narrow goal.

Drucker cites the example of a large Catholic hospital chain in the southwest that decided some years ago to promote the trend of health care moving out of hospitals rather than to fight it. Reasoning that they were in the business of delivering health care to the poor, not running hospitals, the group founded HMOs, laboratory networks, rehabilitation centers, etc. Today, their innovations are largely successful and their hospitals are filled anyway—the freestanding facilities generate all the referrals they need.

If all this sounds suspiciously like an Americanized version of Japanese management theory, it is. The difference is that it has been accomplished not by for-profit corporations that have consciously set out to imitate their Asian competition, but by nonprofit organizations that started with a unified mission and insisted that their strategy (and their personal rewards) flow from their pursuit of it.

Suppose you were asked to evaluate two archers, each of whom used the same equipment to shoot arrows at a target the same distance away, and each of whom hit the bull's-eye an average of 50 percent of the time. Obviously it's a toss-up, unless you happen to learn that one of the archers routinely used a target with a two-inch bull's-eye while the other used a four-inch bull's-eye.

Now take another look at the chart below, reprinted from Chapter 2, We Don't Need to Make a Profit.

INDUSTRY	LOWEST AVERAGE PROFIT	HIGHEST AVERAGE PROFIT
Electric services	2.8%	11.4%
Gas stations	.2%	1.5%
Insurance agents	7.3%	16.8%
Medical laboratories	4.4%	10.3%
Wholesale car parts	.9%	3.5%
Wholesale paper prod- ucts	1.3%	2.5%
Securities brokers	4.0%	18.4%
Building operators and lessors	15.3%	22.9%

(Note: figures are for companies reporting net profits.)
Source: Almanac of Business & Industrial Financial Ratios (Troy, 1990)

Given that most nonprofit organizations are lucky to make a 2 percent profit, who's firing at the smallest bull's-eye here? For-profit executives get to shoot for anything from a few percentage points' profit in lean times to double-digit home runs when times are good. If they fail one year they usually have capital resources to fall back on, plus the option of trying to raise more cash through equity sales. Not only that, they normally have a pretty good say in how to define success from year to year.

Nonprofit executives have none of those advantages. Not only is the functional range of profit permanently much smaller (assuming it's not wiped out entirely by a self-imposed break-even mentality), but few organizations have the capital structure necessary to survive a string of losing years. Nonprofit executives make razor-thin profits because they have to, and they do it year after year. Lee Iacocca did it once and they said he should be in the White House. It's time to start giving yourself and your colleagues credit for the management miracles that otherwise get taken for granted.

What to Do Better

The inescapable fact of all performance evaluation is that you are pronounced a success or a failure by other people. The corollary is that if you can get those other people to view your record favorably early on, you stand an excellent chance of being judged a success in the end.

There are many things you can do to begin influencing public opinion favorably on your behalf and, by extension, on behalf of your peers. One of them is already happening in many organizations and often needs only the slightest encouragement. I am referring to the increasing tendency of nonprofit organizations to hire people with business backgrounds or at least traditional business training for top positions. In other words, say good-bye to the stereotype of the nonprofit executive's credentials as simply a furrowed brow and a year or two of graduate study in something squishy.

It Helps to Speak Both Program and Fiscal

One family service organization I know hired its most recent executive straight out of its national association's central office during the 1970s. When he retired, the board made it clear that they were looking for someone with a business background. The staff, on the other hand, feared that a buttoned-down bean counter would enrich the financials but impoverish the spirit.

Into the breach stepped an executive recruiter's dream: a woman with both an M.S.W. *and* an M.B.A. Originally a child-protective worker, she had decided to study business when she worked at a United Way and felt unable to adequately communicate nonprofit issues to United Way audiences. "I see myself as a bridge between value-based approaches and the demands of business," she says. Another executive with a major regional human services agency is more blunt. "Without a CEO or someone high up with business acumen you're just not going to make it," he says.

There is an undeniable national trend toward the professionalization of nonprofit management. James Clark of ACCESS/Jobs in the Public Interest predicts that charities in the 1990s will be run by a "whole new generation of public-service entrepreneurs, people who realize you have to risk more and you have to be more innovative than we are currently being if we're going to solve problems in both the short and the long term."[3]

It may be subtle, but there is something more profound going on here than simply the for-profit sector losing a few people to the nonprofit side. Drucker is getting at it when he says that many of the executives he teaches complain that in their jobs "there isn't much challenge, not enough achievement, not enough responsibility, and there is no mission, there is only expediency."

Right now there is a cultural gulf between nonprofit and for-profit so large that there is barely even a common language to talk about that fact. The reasons why belong in another book. But as those experienced in American business techniques increasingly find themselves moving in and out of nonprofit settings, both the image of nonprofit management and traditional American business itself will benefit. And for a lot less effort than a pilgrimage to Tokyo.

The Role of Academia

One of the most persistent reasons for nonprofit management's failure to be more highly regarded by the rest of the world is its lack of any real identification with academia. For a look at how a solid tie-in with university education can help a profession soar, we need look no further than physicians.

A century or so ago, physicians enjoyed none of their current prestige, ranking somewhere near the average barber in terms of the public's appreciation of their craft. As recently as the turn of the century, a large portion of medical education was carried out by private, unaffiliated schools with no particularly strong curriculum and large numbers of alumni who tended to say *oops* a lot.

A growing public outcry, culminating in a powerful and persuasive independent investigative report, convinced a majority of the need to reform physician education. As a result, the medical school-university link was forged in some places and greatly strengthened in others. The triangular alliance was completed with the addition of research capabilities in many facilities, and the foundation for what we know as modern medicine was nicely set. By the time federal attention in the form of national medical research and funding for hospital construction were added to the mix later in the century, the profession of physician was on its way to becoming the single most respected and well paid of all the professions.

There is a lesson in the rehabilitation of the reputation of the ordinary doctor here, and it is that the academic link is absolutely essential. (Why else would the number of states allowing lawyers to simply "read for the bar" in lieu of attending classes have declined dramatically during this century?)

Part of the problem for this field in creating or maintaining academic linkages is that the subject matter is hardly homogeneous enough or established enough to become a widespread subject of serious study in its own right. But the entrepreneurial nonprofit executive can do two things to help correct the situation.

One is to establish any kind of academic tie he or she can manage. The obvious one is to teach a course part-time, but there are other ways. For instance, many programs in traditional business management require some sort of internship. Offer a few such students the opportunity to intern at your nonprofit. Even in a general business management environment there are bound to be a few students intrigued by that type of opportunity.

The second way of establishing academic ties is more a way of thinking than a specific strategy, and it is to consciously choose education over training wherever possible. For a variety of reasons, the nonprofit field seems to have its share of training but less than its share of education. Perhaps this is because training tends to come in quick hits that are expected to pay off in improved performance right away, and therefore it is seen as more efficient in the short term. Education, on the other hand, is more of a long-term proposition and amounts to an investment which the average nonprofit feels it cannot or should not make.

The entrepreneurial nonprofit executive will choose education whenever possible, whether as student or teacher. The overarching discipline of an education is far more powerful than the gain of a one- or two-day seminar. Nor should it be an education solely in nonprofit management—the field can be adequately covered by a core set of courses in general management with a few others geared specifically to nonprofit issues. A graduate degree in another discipline with a strong minor in management can be almost as effective.

The combinations are endless, but the consistent theme should be to elevate the status of nonprofit management to a level where academia must take it seriously in one way or another.

Gilt by Association

A tool for communicating one's management prowess that has to be firmly implanted in the choices of every entrepreneurial non-profit executive is membership in key associations. A reality of our industrial society is that communication happens relatively easily up and down in a single organization, but not so easily between organizations, even supposedly noncompetitive nonprofit organizations. Dialogue between industries or between an industry and government is even more difficult.

Facilitating some of these communications is the job of professional associations, and they can be enormously valuable resources for the practicing executive who chooses to use them. More and more executives in both the for-profit and nonprofit sectors are doing just that. On the federal level alone, for instance, there are an estimated fifty thousand trade associations paying careful attention to proposed legislation and regulations. Regionally there are thousands more organizations doing comparable things on a more or less full-time basis. Nonprofit organizations are doing the same thing as well, although our national networks these days are being built from the ground up—by local groups getting together to form regional or statewide associations, and then by those associations tentatively exploring national linkups.

The entrepreneurial nonprofit executive typically belongs to three associations. One is what I call the service-specific association, a formal grouping of nonprofit corporations providing essentially the same service. In practice this level of association is quite likely to be informal with few if any paid staff. Meetings are held periodically and the subject matter tends to be organized around current topics, with the bulk of each session being information exchange and exploration of common experiences of expectation/outcome dissonance (otherwise known as gossiping and griping).

There are also statewide associations to consider. Typically, these groups focus on matters of interest either to a distinct type of nonprofit organization or having to do with the well-being of all nonprofit or charitable agencies. They may be able to provide joint buying programs in addition to their more common research and advocacy efforts.

Finally, every nonprofit executive needs a national perspective. Ideally, it would come from the national counterpart of one of the local groups. As an alternative, it can be one of the excellent nonprofit-oriented associations that have formed in the past several years. Either way, national conferences and publications are a most productive way to divert one's attention from the crush of daily business and spend some time retraining the executive thought muscles.

Do I *Have* to Join the Rotary?

Stop whining. Yes, you have to join the Rotary. Or the Kiwanis. Or the local chamber of commerce. You have a certain amount of choice in the matter, but not much. To make the wisest decision, look around for the largest single collection of prosperous-looking middle-aged white males. Join it. This is as close to the power structure of the community as a voluntary association is likely to let one come, so don't waste any time.

Once inside this group, you will discover two things that surprise you. One is that you will recognize one or two others like you. Whether it is the local museum director or the vice president of the local hospital or the chief financial officer of that large family service agency, there will be at least a smattering of like-minded folks. Especially in rural or suburban areas, it is possible for nonprofit executives to achieve positions of real prom-inence and influence in local groups designed for small businesses. The people I know who have been successful at this sort of thing report with no small amount of satisfaction that their fellow

Rotarians or Chamberites or whatever could just as easily be nonprofit administrators when it comes to discussing their day-to-day challenges.

The second occasion for surprise comes a few months later when you realize that a familiar old saying misses the point—it's not whom you *know* that counts, it's whom you *get to know*. Whom you know is no longer under your control. If you find someone among the list of your past acquaintances who's just the right person for an upcoming situation, it may very well be a fluke. But with a little foresight and some advance planning you can make it a point to start getting to know the people you'll need to know in a few months or a few years. That's where to devote your energy.

And when you stand up at the annual awards dinner five years later to accept the annual achievement award, no one will be surprised.

PART II
THE MONEY

CHAPTER 8

SHHH . . . YOUR MARKET
IS SPEAKING

Let's talk pizza.

When I go into one of my many local pizza shops to order a pizza, the transaction, in economic terms, is pretty simple. It's a two-way exchange of value, as shown below.

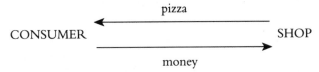

But when I go into one of my (far fewer) local art museums, the transaction is considerably more complex, looking something like this:

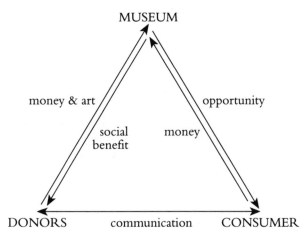

This little diagram is a fair representation of the typical non-profit's performance of mission in economic terms, and it raises some slippery questions. What is the museum's market? Is it the consumer who directly "consumes" the shows? The donors who produce the funding for them? The real transaction is between the artist and me, but it has no economic dimensions. Yet as the consumer I cannot be part of that transaction without entering into the economic ones.

Take another type of transaction familiar to the nonprofit world. Suppose I'm sitting around the house getting bored one night when I decide to take a ride down to the beach with some friends. Only problem is, I'm fifteen years old. And I don't own the car.

And I get arrested.

For the fifth time.

The judge who hears my case and turns me over to a nonprofit youth services organization has set up the following transaction:

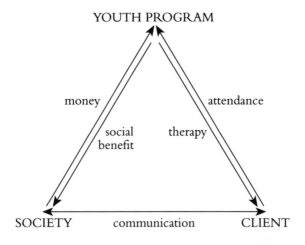

YOUTH PROGRAM

money   attendance

social benefit   therapy

SOCIETY   communication   CLIENT

In this case, society is represented by the judicial system as well as by the source of funds for the youth program. While the only exchange of cash has taken place between some agent of society known as a unit of government and the youth program, for the entire transaction to work properly all elements in the other two sides of the triangle have to be in place too.

Again, the model poses some difficult questions. Is the youth program's market the youth who must contribute his or her attendance, or the vehicle of society that determines which youths get sent there and why? The client may deal with the program on a daily basis, but to what degree is the program merely an embodiment of society's expectations of civilized behavior?

A Matter of Terminology

As executives of business entities, nonprofit administrators must first figure out what their market or markets are. Don't be fooled by terminology here. Many organizations already do this quite skillfully, but call it something different. "Needs assessment" is one popular substitute for the unadorned term "market research." Researching disease prevalence rates and service delivery demand are other more genteel labels for essentially the same activity (incidentally, in my experience, nonprofits often do a far superior job in this area than their for-profit counterparts. If we started calling it "market research" we'd win management awards).

To have a chance at fully grasping the breadth of your market, however, you need to know what it is that your group does well. I call this the process of determining a nonprofit corporation's "core competence" after C. K. Prahalad and Gary Hamel, two authorities who have explored the idea in the for-profit sector.[1]

Essentially, the process of determining an organization's core competencies is nothing more than an attempt to answer the following question: Stripping away cosmetic differences such as industry lingo, geographic location, and administrative peculiarities, what irreducible service(s) is your organization good at providing?

How does one recognize a "core competence"? A core competence is the collective learning of a nonprofit corporation about coordinating diverse skills for specific purposes. It can and should be expressed in a few plain words—if it can't, it's probably not at the "core." Most important, it will almost always be expressed in terms of its effect on the users of the nonprofit's service.

Note that the idea of a core competence is expressed as being located in the corporation, not within individuals working for that corporation. A single teacher, no matter how gifted and effective, does not constitute a core competence. Rather, it derives from the special blend of personal abilities, experience, administrative systems, and collective wisdom that the organization has built up over the years. Although obviously dependent on individuals rather than proprietary technology, the core competence transcends any one individual and promises far more stability for that reason.

Back to Pizza

Go back to that pizza shop for a moment. At first glance, its core competence would appear to be the ability to provide a product desired by many people. But that's not enough to allow the pizza shop owner to think strategically. For one thing, she's not providing a product as much as a service—purchasing and assembling a few simple foodstuffs, then cooking them according to an individual's taste. There is nothing to stop any one customer from doing the same thing at home using commonly available ingredients, and undoubtedly a few do just that. There has to be something unique about this particular shop's pizza, or else it will be replaced by the next shop that opens up nearby.

So what is the shop's core competence? For some hints, look at the environment. It may be, for example, that the shop is the only place where a steady stream of homebound commuters can pick up a quick pizza for dinner, in which case the shop is selling convenience that happens to take the form of pizza. Or it may be the only place for miles around that uses only ingredients imported from Italy, cooks them according to an old family recipe, and serves them in a cozy restaurant with Italian-language music playing. Then its real core competence has more to do with nostalgia and being a cultural anchor than anything culinary. It could just as easily be the favorite gathering place for employees from the neighboring government office building, making the pizza secondary to conducting the informal business of government. And so on.

Whatever the core competence of the pizza shop, someone must take charge of it and do whatever is necessary to preserve it if the organization wants to be around tomorrow. Usually that's exactly what happens, though rarely consciously.

A Small Example

Many years ago I used to supervise small residential programs for chronically mentally ill people. One of the most persistent topics for staff at all levels was the experience of burnout, and underlying that concern was the often unspoken acknowledgment that the work was permanently frustrating. We all rarely felt like we had explicit success, yet there was a widespread feeling both inside and outside the staff that it was a good program. Why didn't we feel better about our work?

The explanation is that our understanding of our core competence was wrong. Rightly or wrongly, we all felt in some way that our job was to "cure" the clients living in the program. In fact, it was hard *not* to feel that way, what with all the emphasis on service planning, client relationship building, and other quasi-clinical activities that our funding source required. Yet few of our clients ever achieved anything even remotely resembling a "cure," so naturally we tended to feel consistently like failures.

An analysis of the type I describe would have shown us that our true competencies had nothing to do with curing mentally ill people. Our core competencies were our abilities to provide 1) decent housing and 2) a safe environment for chronically mentally ill clients. Although many of our clients had had relapses while living at the program, all of them enjoyed decent housing and the program environment was universally respected for its supportiveness and caring atmosphere.

Don't Jump Yet

I would like to say that all nonprofit organizations should carefully and deliberately consider their core competencies and act accordingly. But the reality is that for the chief executive in some agencies to jump into the process would be tantamount to professional suicide. The process of determining core competencies can be painful for some of those involved. If someone had suggested to me and my would-be clinician colleagues back then that our competence rested on providing something as seemingly mundane as a decent place to live and a sense of safety in that living environment, we would have been greatly offended. Never mind that it takes a great deal of skill and talent to provide decent housing and a good atmosphere for chronically mentally ill people—that isn't what we *thought* we were doing. But that is precisely what we were competently providing, and our collective sense of accomplishment and value would have risen greatly if we could have recognized this central fact and organized ourselves accordingly.

It is vital that at least the entrepreneurial nonprofit executive comprehend the corporation's core competencies. In the first place, it gives one a crystal clear focus. More important, it liberates the thought processes. Instead of proceeding from grant to grant, thinking about generating corporate revenue takes on a decidedly broader, entrepreneurial flavor.

I once worked on a consulting team for a medium-sized urban hospital struggling to make its radiology department viable and more integrated with the rest of the hospital. The project took on momentum when we looked back at some of the corporation's original papers and discovered that they talked about delivering health care to the poor and said not one word—*not one word*—about running a hospital. That discovery led us to propose that they explore community-based mammography services, a profound deviation from their normal facility-based way of delivering health care but one which that hospital and many others later routinely followed.

Once the core competence is determined, the next step is to link it with one or more markets by asking, "Who needs this service?" Again, this can be a broadening exercise. One of my favorite human service agencies was a small, struggling foster care agency whose executive director I tried unsuccessfully to convince to figure out their core competence. My theory was that what they were really good at was matchmaking and supporting, and that if they saw themselves in this way it would open up huge new areas for them to explore—match therapist with patient, for example? Open up a human service headhunter program? Match elder volunteers with kids needing guidance? Promising inner city kids with business executives? The possibilities are endless.

Government Funded? Stop Apologizing

A deadening end in this pursuit of market occurs when it runs headlong into government funding. There is a widespread perception that government funding isn't "real," that somehow a program funded largely by government sources is less valid than one that draws most or all of its support from nongovernment sources. If a discussion of your agency's percentage of direct government support has you scuffing your toe and muttering apologies, rethink your position.

Ever hear of Robert Ballard and the crew that discovered the Titanic? A more appealing modern-day band of intrepid explorers is hard to imagine. But have you ever thought of Ballard and his crew as federal employees? Well, as far as I know he's not technically a federal employee, but that crew sailed out of Woods Hole Oceanographic Institute in Massachusetts, and Woods Hole's percentage of government funding is somewhere in the 90s. Yet the last thing you'd associate such a terrific accomplishment with is the federal dollar.

Cheer up, it's all in the image. The government dollar is everywhere in the nonreligious nonprofit field. One survey a few years ago found that 38 percent of all nonhospital nonprofit funding came from government. In my state, the typical percentage of state government support is often double that amount for human service agencies, and the situation is comparable in other states too. Federal funding for the arts is significant and, like federal funding for most services involving nonprofits, is hotly debated from time to time.

In spite of these problems, government funding in certain areas looks like it may grow in the coming years. "Privatization" is the buzzword in some government circles, and it could provide real opportunities for nonprofits. Governments at all levels, especially local and regional, have always used the private sector for certain services, but with further limits on new taxes all over the country, government entities will be looking for creative ways to downsize and purchase services rather than provide them. The entrepreneurial nonprofit executive will be there to answer the call.

Yes, government is a perfectly legitimate "customer" for tax-exempt agencies' services, even if some look down on the transaction. Consider that the real source of this image problem is not that government at all levels funds nonprofit enterprises, but that it does so explicitly. That is one problem with the term tax-exempt—it leaves little to the imagination. For-profit businesses are simply a lot cagier about how they get their funding from government, preferring tax credits and deductions over direct spending.

It's a brilliant strategy. One hundred thousand dollars in legally avoided taxes has the same financial effect on a for-profit business entity as a one hundred thousand dollar direct grant has on a nonprofit, but it has the additional benefit of being harder to pin down and a lot harder for the average person to appreciate. Harvard Professor Stanley Surrey, the Treasury Department's top tax person under President Kennedy and an ardent proponent of tax reform, called the money that for-profit businesses receive from legally avoiding taxes a "tax expenditure" on the part of that government. It's a good term and makes it clear that legally avoided taxes are every bit as much a government expenditure as are government grants and contracts.

Market-Driven Versus Mission-Driven

Without question, the hardest part about getting most nonprofit organizations to think like marketers is that their simple survival doesn't usually depend upon it. On the other hand, the adequate performance of a mission *does* depend on there being at least a modicum of market orientation somewhere in the organization. The apparent discrepancy in this statement derives from the three-party nature of most nonprofit transactions discussed earlier.

There is simply no guarantee of two-way communication between the source of funds and the consumers of the nonprofit services. While it can reasonably be assumed that third parties such as governments and public foundations suffer at worst from a time lag in hearing and processing the message from their relevant consumers that a particular nonprofit service is not working, the fact is that large individual donors are not necessarily concerned with how much the consumer may or may not want the service being funded. Large donations can be created or withdrawn for reasons having nothing to do with the popularity or effectiveness of the proffered service, and this fact can skew their state of being market oriented.

Bring on the Bankruptcies

I would be happier if more nonprofit organizations went out of business. If this sounds strange from someone in my line of work, be assured that it's really not a prescription for any one nonprofit but rather a proposed benchmark that would indicate increased vitality and market consciousness in the field and therefore a tighter link between mission and organizational vehicles.

Depending on whom you believe, between 60 and 80 percent of all for-profit businesses go out of existence within six years of their founding. Does anyone know the equivalent statistic for nonprofits? Based on my personal experience, I would say the percentage is so low it barely interests researchers. There are so few statistics on nonprofit terminations available that we must necessarily rely more on experience and anecdote than hard fact.

Fortunately, for-profit organizations have lots more information readily available, so it's worth taking a look at how they go out of existence for some clues as to why (or how) nonprofits should occasionally follow the same route.

To begin with, let's line up with Bruce Kirchoff, an entrepreneurship professor who prefers to call business terminations "exits" instead of failures. "Failure" is an extremely loaded term, he believes, since some unknown number of companies are closed by owners who reorganize or just move to some new phase in their lives.[2] Stereotypers of business exits paint most of them as entrepreneurial train wrecks, with former owners deep in debt and angry, unpaid creditors fighting it out in bankruptcy court. But in truth only about a quarter of business exits ever reach this stage, most instead proceeding relatively quietly with mutually negotiated settlements. So "exit" is a fairly descriptive term for the most desirable kind of terminations.

Another instructive aspect of business survival, also from Kirchoff, is the role of growth. Or, more exactly, the dangers of staying small. For companies starting with four or fewer employees and adding no new ones in the course of their first six years, the survival rate is only 26 percent. More important, for all companies—of any size at birth—that add no new employees during their first six years, the survival rate is barely more than a percentage point higher.

Those outside the business world overrate the importance of the bottom line in decision making. In many instances, corporations go out of business not because their bottom line in the previous time period was bad (a bit of fast talking can usually explain that away) but because the organization can no longer persuade sources of funds (in every sense of the term) that the future will be any better. The true bottom line is whether outsiders continue to believe in the future of the business.

Quick—before that thought gets lost in the paragraphs that follow—why should organizations exempt from taxation be measured according to a different standard? Why shouldn't nonprofits have exactly the same bottom line? When the donors no longer want to—or can—donate, when the foundations look elsewhere, when government isn't interested, when the banks are afraid to lend—isn't that the time to hang it up as a nonprofit? So why doesn't it happen?

Nonprofits Are Like Old Soldiers

Well, the answer is that it does happen, but not usually with the label "exit" attached. Like old soldiers, nonprofits tend to fade away rather than expire outright. Part of the reason is that we have actually made it rather difficult for nonprofit organizations to go out of business. If you look in the original legal papers setting up the average nonprofit, the chances are that you will find provisions to the effect that assets left over after liabilities have been settled should be distributed to similar organizations doing similar work.

But what are these organizations? How do we know that they are doing similar work? And who will supervise the whole process? Most state attorneys general will probably be inclined to be involved only as a formality, hoping that the private nonprofit sector will work out the details on its own. In any event, regulators' major concern will be that assets acquired through tax-exempt status remain in use for that general type of purpose and not land in sleazy pockets. So there are real administrative disincentives against nonprofits going out of business.

But there is something more profound going on here. A friend of mine found out about it a few years ago. As the executive director of a youth-oriented nonprofit agency, she looked around one day and realized that they were steadily losing ground to the local mental health center. Being a realist, she started talking informally with the mental health center's executive director about merging the two organizations. He was enthusiastic, the fit was right, and she was willing to be the assistant director in the new organization.

When presented with the general idea of a merger the nonprofit's board of directors balked. Not a chance, they said. "But this is our best option to continue the services to kids," she said. "At this rate, without a merger, you'll soon shrink back in size to the original house for runaways." So be it, came the reply.

Another friend calls this the I-Don't-Want-to-Be-Known-as-the-Last-Board-President-of-XYZ syndrome. Board members and staff who have poured so much of themselves into a program are often the most reluctant to see it disbanded, even if the market is calling for it. In this case the motivation, excitement, and energy that are so critical to starting up a program turn into its own worst enemy when the market calls on the corporate vehicle to make major change (within a year, my friend was assistant director of her erstwhile competitor, while her original agency was embarked on a multiyear course of muddling through).

The reason some nonprofit organizations that have lost focus on their mission, or around whom the environment has changed, are allowed to languish is because there is no compelling reason for them to do otherwise. Self-serving or narrow perspectives such as the board's described above take over when there is no broad institutional mission, and as long as there is no effective feedback between funder and consumer, the situation can continue indefinitely.

For a representation of how a nonprofit can lose its market you may need to look no further than your own city or town. Every former church building that is now a day-care center, or condominiums, or is used in some other secular way is an example of what happens when a market changes. It is no accident that religious organizations receive such a large percentage of the individual donations made every year in this country. Religion is very much a two-party transaction, and those groups of worshippers who cannot or will not maintain a church building any longer—or who do things like rallying to rebuild a fire-damaged structure and in the process increase their numbers—are making a market statement about what is important to them.

Nonprofit organizations really have two bottom lines—the one on their financial statements and the one in their mission statement. The bottom line in their financial statements comes first, because without it they won't be around to serve tomorrow. But the real bottom line is whether or not they have accomplished their mission. It's the zeal for accomplishing the mission entrepreneurially that gives the nonprofit the strength to persist over time. And it's the firm expectation of outsiders that the organization will pay attention to its two bottom lines that gives the nonprofit vehicle its unique potency.

Mission First, Corporate Vehicle Second

Every few months someone asks me how to start a nonprofit organization, and my answer usually takes them by surprise: how do they know that they should be choosing the nonprofit form of organization? For that matter, how do they know they should be starting a corporation at all? Perhaps it should be a trust or a partnership, even a single proprietorship or a Subchapter S corporation. The choice of business vehicle should be made on the basis of legal, economic, political, cultural, and financial reasons that will vary greatly in every individual case. But it should be a conscious management choice, not one made instinctively or on the basis of wrong information.

Over time, the payoff of having chosen the right corporate vehicle in the beginning is that it makes it possible to keep the maturing nonprofit's focus exclusively on its mission. With an enduring commitment to keeping mission—client, consumer, patient, etc.—number one, many seemingly sticky questions concerning the fate of any particular corporation or program become easier (or at least less contentious) to answer. If it's right for the mission, details like changes in the corporate structure should be made to follow.

For those squeamish at the thought of thousands of nonprofits flying up to Corporation Heaven, there are alternatives. Foremost among these is merging with another nonprofit. In my part of the country nonprofit mergers are actually old hat, a number of the largest human service nonprofits having been created through mergers in the '50s, '60s, and '70s. But where those mergers tended to have been initiated by funding sources such as United Ways, today's merger talks are started by management.

Unlike those of our for-profit counterparts, nonprofit mergers usually offer no fat consultant fees, no savings to drop to the bottom line, and no reputations to burnish. So, why merge? For one reason only—to strengthen programs. There is a minimum economic size for a given corporation to be able to deliver a given type of service. An art museum has to be large enough to own or somehow control enough space to display and store its works securely and with proper environmental controls. A mental health center needs a sophisticated computer system to track all of its billings and client records. As the complexity of the particular service field increases, the economic size rises and those formerly on the margin find themselves clearly undersized. That's when it's time to merge.

Actually, it's time to merge *before* slipping under the economic size, when it can be done with plenty of planning and implementation time. No one wants damaged goods, and making the decision to merge before circumstances make it for you is the best way to insure that services will continue. One of the best merger decisions I've seen was made by a nursing home that looked at the deteriorating state of its natural client base and realized that at some point in the future it would become little more than a publicly supported warehouse for elderly patients. While still carrying a healthy fund balance and an acceptable mix of publicly supported versus privately paying clients, it sought out a larger nursing home in the same city for merger talks.

Conversely, mergers can be the fastest way for an entrepreneurial nonprofit executive to enlarge his or her agency. Two caveats about growth through merger, though. First, the core competencies of the two agencies must be compatible, or else they will find themselves working against each other. Second, the dominant culture will always survive, meaning that top management and committed veterans of the weaker-cultured agency will either leave soon after the merger or be miscast in the new environment.

Rambo Fund Raising

For a population which on the whole I have found to consist of an unusually large number of gentle souls, many nonprofit executives have an oddly confrontational theme underlying much of their fund-raising pitch. In fact, it's downright threatening:

> "*You better donate to us* [Or else we'll have to close down and then we'll blame you]."

This is no mere threat, it's a full-scale assault by the Guilt Commandos. Never mind that the attack is usually repelled with a minimal amount of ease, it's still an effort to reach wallets via superegos, a contorted approach unlikely to work.

What's revealing about this style is what my psychologist friends might call its inner-directedness. It really talks only about the recipient's needs, and it even does that in an indirect and

unsatisfying way. It overlooks the fact that the nonprofit manager's large and terrifying reality of needing more money doesn't
even show up as a blip on the rest of the world's radar screen. It's
not that the rest of the world doesn't care, of course—just that it
doesn't have any particular reason for caring.

On the other hand, if you can show how it is in your market's
own interest to contribute, you present a much stronger case.
Doing so requires that you and the organization focus outward,
on your environment's needs, not on your own, and it demands a
much different orientation from the one normally found in a
professional setting.

Most highly trained professionals naturally focus on the objects
of service that have in some way already entered into the organization. Teachers, for example, concentrate on enrolled students,
doctors on admitted patients, social workers on accepted clients,
etc. By training and (usually) by personal preference, their energies go to those who have somehow passed into their institutions,
otherwise known as patients, clients, etc. But, by definition, the
organization's market is outside the system, and that is where
marketing energies must be directed.

This is one of the reasons why many professionals are lousy
marketers. Successful marketing implies doing things so dramatically differently that many cannot make the transition. These
tendencies are so ingrained in professionals' training and practice
that a bona fide professional with solid marketing sense often is
such a standout that he or she becomes the most powerful senior
manager in a nonprofit hierarchy.

Another mistake many professionals make is to confuse selling
with marketing. Selling is actually a fairly low-level activity in the
sense that it consists chiefly of offering to the customer what the
institution already has on the shelf, while marketing looks outside
the institution to find out what people would like to see on that
shelf and then tries to put it there. "The aim of marketing," writes
Peter Drucker, "is to make selling superfluous."[3] Good marketing
turns salespeople into order takers and decision assisters.

Not surprisingly, professional services are almost always mar-
keted rather than sold. Like every other business entity, nonprofit
corporations have a constituency for their professional services

that must be satisfied. Entrepreneurial nonprofit executives recognize this reality even if they don't always put in into words. In fact, they normally don't put much of anything into words. They don't have time. They're too busy listening.

CHAPTER 9

TO OWN OR NOT TO OWN, AND OTHER SILLY QUESTIONS

Adequate capitalization is not a phrase found in most nonprofit managers' vocabulary. Maybe it should be. If there is such a thing as a nearly invisible key to any type of nonprofit's long-term survival as an entity, it is the ability to acquire and hold tangible assets over the long term. Being adequately capitalized is the difference between controlling one's economic fate and being controlled by circumstances.

The image—and the reality—of the nonprofit organization as perpetually struggling to stay afloat financially is in large measure a product of policies and practices that neglect the capital development of the agency. Many of the problems that masquerade as day-to-day-operational challenges can be traced directly back to inadequate capitalization. The happy part is that a bit of studied attention to this area pays dividends literally and figuratively, and that the first step is nothing more expensive than shaping the right attitude.

Capital Is Not a Four-Letter Word

All you residual Marxists, step to the rear. The spirit of capitalism is every bit as alive in the successful nonprofit as it is in the heart of Wall Street, though it may go by a different name (collections instead of inventory, fund balance in place of owner's equity, etc.).

89

To get some inkling of what it means to be adequately capitalized, haul out your most recent financial statements. Look for the balance sheet and then find the number for total assets.

Now look for the total of the money owed you as of the date of the statement. This is the figure for accounts receivable. Divide it by the number for total agency assets. The resulting percentage helps tell how much of certain things of value owned by the agency (accounts receivable) are currently under the control of someone else. The reckoning here is fairly simple: the higher your percentage of tangible assets, the closer you are to being a sequoia among saplings. The lower the percentage, the closer you are to a seedling. By the way, keep the balance sheet handy, you'll need it later.

Often the single largest category of expense for a nonprofit after personnel costs is occupancy, and it is here that one can see the effects of differing policies regarding capitalization. And perhaps the easiest way to see the advantages to owning over renting is to compare two hypothetical nonprofit agencies, one that owns its own facility and one that rents.

The chart at left shows just such a comparison for the first three years and then for the sixth year. The differences are dramatic and educational.

First, a word or two of explanation about the chart. It is intended to show only the costs that would differ materially according to whether the property is being rented or owned. For example, routine maintenance and repair is missing from both ownership and rental because the facility is presumed to be newly constructed/renovated at the beginning and because any maintenance or repair expense would cost Agency A the owner the same as Agency B the renter. Of course, Agency A's landlord may well tack on a little extra profit as he passes the cost of the repair on to Agency A, but that is assumed not to happen for the purposes of analysis. The cost of utilities and minor repairs for the actual user of the property should also be the same in either case.

Finally, we have assumed an acquisition cost of $250,000 for the property, with modest rates of growth in both real estate taxes and appreciation each year.

RENT VERSUS OWN COMPARISON

	YEAR 1	YEAR 2	YEAR 3	YEAR 6
General:				
Real Estate Appreciation	0.0%	5.0%	5.0%	8.0%
Tax Rate Per Thousand	17.50	17.50	18.00	19.25
Land & Buildings at Cost	$250,000	$250,000	$250,000	$250,000
L & B Tax Assessed Value	$250,000	$262,500	$275,625	$337,563
Components of Rent (Agency A):				
Depreciation	$25,000	$25,000	$25,000	$25,000
Interest	$19,582	$19,582	$19,582	$19,582
Taxes	$4,375	$4,594	$4,961	$6,498
Rent Subtotal	$48,957	$49,176	$49,543	$51,080
Profit	$4,896	$4,918	$4,954	$5,108
Total Rent	$53,853	$54,094	$54,497	$56,188
Components of Ownership (Agency B):				
Depreciation	$11,500	$11,500	$11,500	$11,500
Interest	$32,000	$32,361	$31,782	$26,456
Total Cost of Ownership	$43,500	$43,861	$43,282	$37,956
Rent Less Own	$10,353	$10,233	$11,215	$18,232
Cumulative Ownership Benefits to Agency B	$10,353	$20,586	$31,801	$77,872

Why the Landlord Charges More

Right away you can see many of the reasons why renting costs more. Private landlords, for example, will depreciate their property as rapidly as the tax law will allow them to. The overall effect of speeding up the process of acquiring unencumbered ownership of the property is that the yearly cost will be higher.

Tax-exempt organizations, on the other hand, especially those receiving substantial amounts of government funding in a fiscally regulated environment, must often accept drawn-out depreciation schedules. While this increases interest costs, it obviously limits depreciation as an expense. In addition, sharp-eyed regulatory analysts often refuse to allow depreciation on land altogether, thereby reducing allowable depreciation even further. The net effect in our model is to make the cost of covering these basic components of property ownership slightly higher for the rental option.

An even more interesting flip happens as the tax-exempt organization renting its property starts paying taxes. Canny landlords will build the cost of real estate taxes into the first year's rent and then charge the tax-exempt tenant the amount by which taxes increase each succeeding year. It's a perfectly legal strategy (they do it with taxable tenants too), but a waste of a tax exemption.

And then there's profit. Here, our landlord adds a perfectly reasonable 10 percent profit onto his basic property costs. A large corporate landlord would build in a factor to cover some of its overhead costs too, so its deal would be that much more expensive. Why not keep that profit in the organization and use it for just about anything else?

When the dust settles at the end of Year One in our model, property-owning Agency B has netted ownership benefits of $10,353, a figure which grows steadily to a cumulative $77,872 at the end of Year Six.

Wait, There's More

Adequately capitalizing operations benefits a nonprofit organization beyond simple short- and long-term savings. Any business entity, for-profit or nonprofit, needs access to capital in order to come into being, stabilize, and grow. A proprietary corporation might get its first infusion of capital from the owner's pocket, a nonprofit from the proceeds of a bake sale (or a bequest, a grant, etc.).

In any event, the source is not nearly as important as is the common practice of using the money to hire, buy, rent, or lease whatever is necessary to get things rolling. Once underway, either type of corporation can generate capital by accumulating internal profits. The difference is that capital invested in a for-profit in the form of owner's equity, loans, stocks, or bonds theoretically can be taken back virtually any time the owner desires. Since a nonprofit corporation by definition can have no stockholders or owners, its access to capital is more limited. Further, once the money is in the organization, it cannot be returned to the investor.

Putting all of these pieces together leaves the average nonprofit organization with only a handful of ways of raising capital to put an adequate foundation under its operations; internal profits, grants, loans, and bonds.

Predictably, there are problems with each source. Loans and bonds, especially those obtained with market or above-market rates of interest, bring dollars into the organization but by themselves do nothing to help the agency permanently. In fact, if an agency has insufficient success creating profits or securing unrestricted grants to help increase its fund balance, loaned capital can actually be quite dangerous. Over time, if the agency repeatedly breaks even or loses money, it has to borrow more and more money at ever higher rates until eventually it becomes unattractive to any bank at any price.

Even for agencies regularly turning a profit, a high degree of borrowing is a high-risk strategy. The interest on borrowing is essentially a fixed expense, and until it can be comfortably covered with existing operations, it locks the borrowing agency into a future direction that can be summed up in one word: *more*. As long as revenue keeps increasing, the fixed interest expense shrinks as a percentage of overall spending; but once the revenue levels off or starts heading down, the choices become painful.

One of my favorite nonprofit executives used high leverage as a very successful strategy. Having taken a small nonprofit and hurled it from the 1960s into the 1990s, he incurred long-term debt six times his agency's cumulative fund balance, with seven cents of every incoming dollar being spent on interest charges. Fortunately—and not coincidentally, I might add—his agency was innovative and well organized in a growing field, so that after a small boom in real estate prices caused his agency's properties to appreciate nicely they were out of the danger zone. Of course, had the agency's fortunes suffered a downturn in the interim, my friend would probably be in a different line of work today.

If there is a central organizing principle behind Western business, including most nonprofits, it is that executives get paid according to their routine proximity to decisions about how to use capital. Solving the capitalization riddle, in other words, is at the heart of successful nonprofit entrepreneurialism.

Nonprofit executives have special pluses and minuses operating for them as they wrestle with the question of capitalization. On the plus side, no other business entities are given money with no expectation of giving something proportionately valuable and concrete in return. Yet that is exactly what happens every time a nonprofit organization receives an unrestricted donation, grant, or bequest. Not only do these unique sources of capital mean an increase in overall capitalization, but they're interest-free as far as official accounting records go, or at least extremely inexpensive if you factor in the cost of the staff time spent in securing them.

This is why income from unrestricted bequests should never be used for day-to-day expenses until the agency has achieved its capital goals. Bequests as a source of revenue are an unreliable income stream anyway, but perhaps the most insidious aspect of relying on bequests for any substantial portion of yearly income is that such a strategy is fundamentally passive. Even for agencies with a large enough pool of potential donors that the laws of probability smooth out yearly fluctuations, the message that it sends is Tin Cupism at its worst, making the agency dependent on the most profoundly uncontrollable events in its environment.

Weigh Your Capital

To flirt with the possibility of real surprise, and to learn something about your agency's de facto capitalization policies, calculate your weighted average cost of capital. (And do it yourself—no delegating on this one). It's simpler than it sounds.

First, take out your balance sheet again. This time, find the section for liabilities. On a blank sheet of paper, copy down each line item in the liabilities section. These lines represent the sources of claims by various outsiders against the assets of the organization. Make space for three columns. In the first column, calculate what percentage of total liabilities each line item represents. In the second column, put down the interest rate associated with each source of liability.

This is the difficult part, so refer to the example below for suggestions about how to value the interest rate if it isn't explicitly stated somewhere. Accounts payable and accrued payroll are easy; no one charges the organization interest for these outstanding liabilities. The money you owe employees for vacation time is interest-free, a kind of loaned time. Ignore the vendors who charge a penalty for late payment unless you routinely pay all vendors late and incur the penalty often. In that case, you can probably assume that late payment translates into a yearly interest rate of 15 to 20 percent or more, so put that down. Late payment penalties are really an expensive form of interest.

If you have a short-term loan, put the cost of its interest in the second column. Same story with a long-term loan and a mortgage (use the interest rate in effect for the twelve months covered by the balance sheet if a loan rate is adjustable). It will get a bit complicated if the agency has a variety of small, short-term loans outstanding, such as for motor vehicles or equipment purchases. In that case, calculate the percentage of total notes outstanding that each year's worth of loaned capital represents, then multiply it by the interest rate on that loan. Add the individual numbers together for a composite rate of interest paid on loans.

Valuing the cost of the fund balance as a source of capital is a matter of judgment. While it can be argued that the money costs nothing to use, most managers agree that there is a real cost for using internal funds in this way. Putting a number on their worth is a different story. One reasonable answer is to value the funds at the rate that one must pass up in order to use them on the project at hand. The jargon for this is the opportunity cost of the money. So if investments normally available to the organization produce,

SAMPLE CALCULATION OF COST OF CAPITAL

Liabilities	Amount x	Rate x	Fraction of Total	Cost of Source
A/P & Accrued Expenses	$254,716	0	0.12	0.0
Note Payable	$229,056	10.5*	0.10	1.1
Mortgages Payable	$994,580	11.2	0.45	5.0
Fund Balance	$723,903	8.0	0.33	2.6
Totals	$2,202,255		1.00	8.7

*From notes to financial statement.

say, 8 percent revenue, then use 8 percent as the so-called cost of fund balance financing.

Now multiply each item in the first column by its counterpart in the second to arrive at the weighted rate. Total the weighted rates for an overall average cost of capital. *This is the cost of capital your policies have produced.* The lower it is, the better your sources of capital. Since a number of the elements charge no interest (accrued payroll, for example), the weighted average cost of capital ought to be lower than could be obtained through official financing. The higher the number, the more expensive your capitalization policies are.

The central point to remember in all of this is that capitalization choices are real and should be made with an overall policy in mind. Decisions about how to use capital are at the heart of the entrepreneurial nonprofit executive's job, even if it doesn't seem that way at times. An adequate program of capitalization can literally be the foundation for an entrepreneurial agency.

CHAPTER 10

HOW TO GET OFF YOUR KNEES AND STILL GET THE LOAN

This is your banker.

Your banker is smiling.

Is it because he is happy that you are having this discussion about your cash flow needs this morning? Not exactly. Your banker is never truly happy when discussing your cash flow needs. Or your property purchasing needs, for that matter. Even though your banker is smiling, he is not genuinely happy. In fact, your banker is a great deal less than happy. If you look deep into his eyes you will see what he is really feeling: *Terror.*

Why does your banker feel this way? It's really very simple. You see, of all his customers, you are the only one who could cause the following headline to appear in the local newspaper:

FIRST HEARTLESS BANK AND TRUST
FORECLOSES ON MOTHER CLARA'S ORPHANAGE!!

How would you like to be the promising young loan officer responsible for Mother Clara's account the morning that headline appears? That job with the First National Bank of Istanbul would suddenly look a lot more appealing.

I exaggerate. But only a little. For both bankers and their regulators, the written rules governing banking practices are a bit different when it comes to tax-exempt organizations. There is a tacit agreement between government regulators and the banks they regulate that the average nonprofit agency, especially one with strong community ties, gets different regulatory consideration.

Most nonprofit organizations don't realize that they have a decided advantage over the ordinary customer when it comes to keeping a bank's attention. The real issue for most managers is finding the right bank in the first place.

Think Like a Lender

Ironically, your success as a borrower will improve measurably if you think like a lender. It's not as painful as it sounds, and it can pay off very quickly.

The first step in thinking like a lender is to understand that bankers are seeking one thing from you—an annuity. That is, they are looking to commit you to paying them regular amounts each month for a certain number of months. Call it a loan or a mortgage or whatever else you want to, what it amounts to is a stream of cash the banker can count on each month. Anything that assists that stream of cash or predicts it or makes it more likely to come in is good. Anything that interferes with it or makes it less likely to come in is bad.

What the banker gives in return for that annuity is access to other people's capital. Unlike insurance companies, bankers offer steady access to capital without preconditions such as an unexpected loss. Like insurance companies, there are many different layers and levels of capital, and it pays to know how they all work.

Think of banks as a front office and a back office. The front office is the one you see, busily accepting money for deposit, making loans, and offering financing programs of various types. In the back office, they're doing something entirely different. Each loan that the front office makes is really an asset of the bank—an annuity that is worth a certain amount and under the right circumstances can be transferred to another institution. The back office's job is to figure out ways of making those loans as profitable as possible for the bank.

As you might imagine, the less effort the back office needs to put into a given deal, the happier it is. To the people in the back office, their time is worth money, and everybody is happier if they don't have to spend much time on a single loan. Even better, if bunches of the same kind of loan can be put together and sold to other financial institutions like bonds, the back office will happily structure its operations that way. The less conventional the loan or the borrower, the less that back office really understands it, and the less they understand something, the less they like it.

Each loan lands somewhere on the continuum between cookie cutter on one end and quirky on the other. The quirkier the loan, the more likely the bank is to keep it for itself or perhaps even to regard it as a form of community service. The more like a cookie cutter shape a loan is, the more appealing it may be to another institution. The entrepreneurial nonprofit executive makes a point of finding out what his or her banker would like to do with the loan.

The real hidden story behind banks and bankers is regulation. Without some form of regulation, it would be possible for an institution to go off merrily writing loans until it ran out of typewriter ribbon. But the bank's service is to offer its customers access to capital, and unfettered loan writing would eventually result in offering access to capital that didn't exist anymore.

Government regulators try to compensate for this danger by requiring banks to keep a certain amount of reserves, or liabilities, to partially offset the loans they report as assets. By changing reserve requirements, regulators can affect the lending policies of the regulated banks. Off the record, banking professionals will acknowledge that this is one of the areas from which a bank's nonprofit business is tacitly exempted, so it seems irrelevant to the borrowing success of nonprofits. When times are good and reserve requirements are acceptable to the banks, nonprofits will get their share of credit. But few tax-exempt agencies are likely to make their bank's short list of most favored customers when credit policies get tight, so there is definitely an indirect effect.

There's a funny thing about banking consumer behavior. Today we get our news from nationwide television networks, we drive our cars on a monumental interstate highway system, and we purchase hundreds of products from national retail chains, all three systems having gotten established only since mid-century. Yet when it comes to choosing a banker we act as though we're picking out a character for a Norman Rockwell painting.

Outside of the infamous savings and loan failures, there are two banking stories of the '90s that the entrepreneurial nonprofit executive will follow. One is the reshuffling of our banking system, and the other is the public fortunes of that system's managers. In today's world of global capital exchange and electronic fund transfers, the stand-alone Mom and Pop bank is a relic of the past. And often an expensive one, at that. We all may wish otherwise, but the locus of control of most consumer-oriented banks has shifted away from the community in which the bank is physically located. For the large nonprofit corporation, this means that its representatives must move in different circles in order to get closer to the bank's decision makers. For smaller nonprofits, it's one more piece tending to push them toward growth as a means of insuring greater stability.

The second story about bankers in the coming decade is that they are on their way to joining lobbyists and management consultants as a despised professional minority. For the ever-vigilant nonprofit executive, this trend means opportunity. After having its local image kicked around by a scandal or two, what bank wouldn't like to show its civic-mindedness by entering into a well-publicized relationship with the nonprofit down the street? A picture in the local newspaper or even a mention on the sign touting the nonprofit's new bank-financed building project could be worth a dozen damage control press releases.

What It Will Cost

Another aspect of the borrowing game you need to understand is how the bank thinks about its pricing. In the end, it considers three elements: risk, labor, and profit. Risk is the bank's assessment of interference with that future stream of cash they seek. Labor is the amount of time and energy the bank spends administering your account. Profit is the bank's targeted return. Let's take each element individually to see what you can affect and how you can affect it.

How Do You Spell R-I-S-K?

Naturally, assessing risk is a very subjective activity. It is also probably the single most malleable element in a nonprofit's pricing equation, and the one that is easiest to manipulate in your favor.

Since we all tend to fear things we don't understand, your first job is to make your banker understand what you do. Assume he or she knows nothing about your field (a safe assumption), and start at the beginning. Better still, find a bank with experience and interest in lending to your type of organization. If you can, get the people involved to come out to your site for a personal tour, especially if you have no imminent plans to borrow. And do it routinely, not just in the middle of a financial pinch.

When it comes time to do some serious borrowing, what your banker needs to know is where his or her loan fits into your scheme of things. He or she will ask for your most recent audited financial statements, your budget, cash flow projections, and possibly other information as well. Give them willingly. Your banker wants to know whether you have the assets to collateralize the loan, the cash flow to cover it, and the fiscal health to afford it. That's how he spells r-i-s-k r-e-d-u-c-t-i-o-n.

Another way to lubricate the lending machinery is to find out how the bank will "grade" your application. Most banks routinely use computer software programs to assess financial information and make rough predictions about where you are going to be at the end of your proposed loan's term. Ask them which software package they plan to use. There are only about a half-dozen on the market today, and they should be available from your local software store. If the bank won't reveal the name of its package, and you are seeking extensive credit, you might want to pick one up anyway just to see if it could suggest ways of improving your overall presentation.

The Labor Factor

Answer this question: If you were a bank executive and you had the choice, would you rather lend: a) ten different parties one hundred thousand dollars each, or b) one party a million dollars?

If you answered b, you have what it takes to be a bank executive (but don't consider switching careers—these days, banking is a lot less fun than whatever you're doing). Of course you'd rather make a single million-dollar loan than ten loans one-tenth that size. Even if the risk is absolutely identical, the amount of sheer paperwork that goes into the package of smaller loans is enough to tip the balance. Similarly, the ten-loan package is a lot more attractive than one hundred loans of ten thousand dollars each. And so on.

Even while you speak, your banker is pondering how many hours of his or her time your loan request will take up, how much secretarial time and filing costs it will necessitate, and so on. To some extent, economics are against you on this count. Your loan request is going to take a certain amount of time to process, and you are unlikely to be borrowing an amount measured high enough in the fiscal stratosphere that it will overshadow the inevitable drudgery and its cost.

However, it's possible to win at least some of this battle. Acknowledge that you understand the administrative costs involved in the transaction, and make it clear that you will do your part to keep the paperwork flowing smoothly. That means assuring the bank that you will submit clean and workable financial statements, turn around documentation requests speedily, and so forth. Then, do it. The payoff comes the next time you need to borrow and you can sense a little bit of warm, fuzzy feeling beneath all that banker worsted.

The P Word

Finally, we have the matter of bank profit, or, as it is euphemistically called, margin. How much more than the cost of servicing the loan plus a premium for risk does your banker want? You may already have won here without trying very hard. In my experience the sight of a legitimate, responsible nonprofit (especially a public charity) tends to dampen many bankers' profit motive.

This is not to say that the deal you get will be a good one. The halo effect of your tax status and presumed good works in this context tends to mean that you will get the credit, perhaps at a hefty price, even if the bank's formula's evaluation might otherwise make you unattractive at any price.

Again, a forthright discussion of the bank's needs may help. Not only does such a discussion help clarify the immediate problem, it also marks you as a nonprofit executive who is comfortable with business matters, always a useful distinction and one which your banker will probably think right up until that moment is a contradiction in terms.

The B Word

One of the most encouraging developments in small to medium-sized nonprofit financing is the recognition that banks aren't the only place to raise money. Exhibit A in this case is the bond market, which in some parts of the country has discovered that small to medium-sized nonprofit organizations can be decent business partners.

From the bond market's point of view, our story begins in Washington. For years, a great deal of housing and economic development was carried out using tax-exempt bonds issued through some level of government or a quasi-governmental authority. But congressional types, especially staffers, were never really comfortable with all that tax-free business assisting indirectly with private gain. And so there began a gradual process of chipping away at tax-exempt bonding authority as it supported private business, culminating with tax reform legislation in 1984 and 1986 that closed off whole segments of a formerly active financing market.

Naturally, bond and capital finance types began looking elsewhere for fertile deal-making ground, increasingly mindful of the fact that tax-exempt financing to tax-exempt organizations offered bondholders essentially the same advantages as the tax-exempt bonds of for-profits. At about this same time, small to medium-sized nonprofit corporations were beginning to increase their financial savvy dramatically. Investment instruments in general were undergoing unprecedented rounds of innovation—one financier I know talked of routine business dealings with investment banking firms that were deriving 60 percent of their income from financial vehicles that hadn't even existed five years before. Most important of all, new foreign capital was arriving on our shore looking for ways to invest itself in the American system.

What we had was a recipe for positive change, and it has been happening. In my state alone, over fifty million dollars worth of capital financing was issued in two years to nonprofits that had formerly been completely shut out of the capital finance mainstream. Two quasi-public bonding authorities actually began fighting with each other over which was the more natural agent to service the new market.

The benefits of bond-based financing for the average nonprofit organization are many. First of all, it is usually cheaper than conventional bank financing, and unlike some loans with local banks, cannot be pulled back at the lender's pleasure. Just completing the exercise of a bond offering can impose a kind of discipline on an organization that should improve planning for the project being financed (part of the bond issuance process involves putting together a descriptive document as thick as the average paperback bestseller and twice as complicated).

The disadvantages derive from the economics of a bond issue. Costs of professional services related to issuing a bond can easily run into six figures, and factoring that cost into the interest cost and principal repayment of the bond itself can significantly boost the actual cost of borrowing. Consequently, the issuing organization and its project have to be of a certain minimum size in order to make the deal work. Rarely will an individual bond be issued for less than two million dollars, and usually everyone involved is more comfortable if the bond is well over that amount.

Pooling borrowers is the solution of choice for this dilemma. Putting together a group of borrowers with similar characteristics such as service type, financial profile, and geography has the advantage of giving each participating nonprofit access to an otherwise closed capital market in a format that is acceptable to bond issuers and buyers. It requires a bit more coordination and flexibility on everyone's part, but it can be done.

Check that banker suit hanging in your closet. Are the knees wearing faster than the seat? Do your best nylons need replacing after a trip to the money people? If the answer is yes, throw them away and start over again. Make deals, not apologies.

CHAPTER 11

LIABILITY INSURANCE: COVERING YOUR ASSETS WITHOUT LOSING YOUR SHIRT

To the list of life's unpleasant certainties, just below death and above taxes, most nonprofit managers would enthusiastically insert dealing with liability insurance. This is unfortunate, because if there is one part of a nonprofit's operations likely to benefit from some close scrutiny, this is the one. Here are some things to keep in mind when it's time to cover your agency's valuables.

You're Not Stupid, It Really *Is* Confusing

What is it about liability insurance that can give otherwise self-confident and knowledgeable senior nonprofit managers fits of self-doubt and indecision? The short answer: the same thing that leads everybody else—including many in the insurance business— to the same state. In this country there are nearly four thousand companies selling property and casualty insurance alone, and scores of times that many insurance agencies. Add to that the sheer quantity and variety of nonprofit organizations potentially seeking liability insurance (in my state alone there are more than twenty-nine thousand), and you have the makings of a nearly incomprehensible mess.

One of my most memorable experiences in this area occurred when I sat on the steering committee of a local United Way's effort to explore what could be done about the liability insurance crisis in the mid-'80s. The headquarters of a nationally recognized,

109

high-powered business consulting firm donated an entire team of consultants to staff the project. At the first meeting these apple-cheeked, superbly talented MBAs confidently explained their intended approach, which had worked magic since the firm first began operations. They would search out the best methods of coping with all the various aspects of the liability insurance crisis, they said, then assemble the best methods into a single overall recommended practice.

Six months later, we had our final meeting, and these poor wretches with sunken cheeks explained that they had been unable to categorize their two hundred-agency sample in anything even resembling a meaningful way. The closest they could come was to compare the liability insurance coverage of three boys' and girls' clubs. Worse, even in their three-agency sample they had been utterly unable to make any sense of the practices. The organization paying the most did not necessarily have the best coverage, and the organization with the best coverage yielded no insight into how others could replicate their success.

We thanked them graciously for their hard work and sent them on their way, silently hoping that their next assignment would be easier—say, a leveraged buyout.

Insurance Is a Financial Service

Like many complicated fields, insurance seems surrounded by an impenetrable fog of complexity. You can cut through this fog for your own agency by constantly reminding yourself that insurance is nothing more than a financial service. Just as surely as lending money is a financial service, so is promising access to money in the event that certain conditions occur. Therefore, there is no single "correct" answer to the question, "How much insurance is enough?" since the degree of risk and the financial protection required vary from nonprofit to nonprofit. Your goal should be to protect your agency's assets, both those on the balance sheet and the ones that can't be quantified, such as community image and credibility.

Think of your need for insurance as a service that can be

provided by two different parties: your nonprofit agency, and a company or companies in the business of promising access to their capital. The more capital you have access to, the less access you will need to someone else's and the lower your insurance cost can be. It is no accident that many for-profit companies diminish or entirely eliminate their need for this financial service by setting up their own insurance "company" or by setting aside a part of their capital to self-insure their own risks. As we better understand the need for adequately capitalized nonprofit operations, and then act upon that improved understanding, there may come a day when nonprofits routinely opt out of the traditional insurance market in large numbers.

Ride the Insurance Cycle

Another certainty about the insurance world is that boom follows bust and bust follows boom. Chart the profitability of the liability insurance industry over time, and you will see wild swings from mind-boggling profits to mind-boggling operating losses. Of course, the catch is that boom for the companies is bust for you, and vice versa. The trick for the individual agency is to be able to judge which way the tide is flowing and go along with it. Here is what the insurance cycle looks like from your point of view and from the insurance companies':

What You See	What Your Insurance Company Sees
Crisis: Insurance is scarce, prices soar, and no one selling insurance will even return your phone calls. Stay with whatever company you have and hope you don't get a nonrenewal letter.	Revenue and profits look better than they have for a while; Wall Street is in love again.
Prices aren't rising as fast, but they sure aren't coming down either. Hang on, the best is yet to come.	The best of times, the highest of profits; insurance company CEOs start appearing on the covers of business magazines.

An upturn. Expect better pricing soon, and start looking around if you want to change insurance companies.

Find a good deal and cement it; bargain hard on price. This is the payoff for your earlier patience.

New investors pump in a few billion dollars, but the party was over before they heard about it.

Crisis: Losses are soaring, investment returns are sagging. It's obvious that the average insurance company CEO couldn't manage a one-car funeral.

The Two Faces of Insurance

Successfully surfing the insurance company waves is more complicated than just figuring out where you stand in the process and then making a move or staying put. Frankly, this is because most insurance company executives don't have the slightest idea what you do, and if you're a small or medium-sized nonprofit organization, you probably don't pay enough premium dollars to make them want to learn.

Divide the insurance company world into two types. For our purposes, the first type of company might be called the household names. These are the groups that everyone knows because they've been around so long or because they advertise widely. If something is familiar or there's lots of it, they'll insure it. These companies insure cars, hotels, buildings, people's lives, manufacturing equipment, and just about anything else you might expect to run into during the ordinary course of things.

Of course, there's more to insure beyond the stuff of everyday life. If your company runs fifty-ton transport barges in and out of East Coast harbors—or if you operate a day-care center—the chances are pretty good that the household names won't be terribly interested in you. That's where the surplus lines insurance companies get into the picture. These are the less well-known companies that play around the fringes of the insurance world by selecting one or more specialized types of businesses to insure or by sharing certain types of insurance responsibilities with other companies.

While the insurance contract with either type of company can be equally valid, the two types behave differently under different circumstances, and this can have an effect on you as a consumer. For example, in the liability insurance crises of the mid-1980s many nonprofit organizations insured by the surplus lines companies found themselves holding very expensive pieces of paper stamped "insurance policy" as their insurance companies were fatally injured on the insurance cycle. This drove nonprofits into the not necessarily open arms of the household name companies. For their part, the household names were also interested in retrenching, so they rarely took on any new nonprofit business and even dumped some existing clusters of nonprofits (and others) on occasion. True to form, when the market got better for consumers ("softened" is the jargon), some of both types of companies got interested again. Be sure you know which type of company you're using.

Who Really Holds the Purse Strings

Another important way to divide up the insurance world for the purpose of understanding it better is by primary insurers or reinsurers. Picture your insurance company as a single-story brick storefront. Insurance company people are busily accepting your premiums, investing your money, and generally doing the things that insurance companies do. Periodically, when they realize that the amount of risk they are exposed to has built up beyond what they consider an acceptable level, one of the top executives puts on his coat, goes out the back door, and hops a plane to some faraway city where he proceeds to buy an enormous insurance policy for his own insurance company. His mission accomplished—and his own company's wallet lighter by a few million— our friend returns home and gives the signal to start selling insurance again.

This is how reinsurance works, and it is one of the most profound influences on who gets insured, how, and for how much. In many lines of insurance, the real power and risk is held by reinsurance companies while the insurance company that we know and love is more like an administrative unit holding only a part of the risk represented by the policy. The most famous source of reinsurance is Lloyd's of London, which people think of as an insurance company although it is more akin to a stock market in which hundreds of people agree to cover a small piece of a big risk in return for the possibility of collecting their share of a fat premium.

Since primary insurance companies can lay off a good portion of their risk on reinsurance companies, these upstream behemoths have a good deal to say about how the companies you and I know decide to do things. And since they tend to operate in a world where one rounds numbers to the nearest million, the chances are slim that they have much firsthand information about your type of tax-exempt agency.

For this reason, the most important move you can make in managing your insurance coverage is to select an agent and, if possible, a company familiar with nonprofit organizations as well as your particular field. When at least one of the other parties talks your language the communication is more efficient. More important, it may mean that the agent or the company has enough other similar organizations, and that together you're big enough to get recognized when necessary. Economies achieved this way can make marketing simpler and therefore help cut down on the agent's fee—especially if you suggest it.

How to Rate Them

Fortunately for consumers, the people who monitor and evaluate insurance companies must have enjoyed grammar school, because they created a system of rating the companies that even a third grader would understand—A+ through C. It's called the Best Ratings, and they are the single most authoritative guide to the performance and expected reliability of American insurance companies. Put out by the A. M. Best Company in New Jersey, the rating applied to each company in the liability insurance field is the most popular of its kind. The company's Best letter means exactly what that letter meant in school, although it should also be noted that there can be some legitimate if deeply technical reasons why Best would refuse to rate a company even though it was fiscally adequate.

You Are a Commercial Account

Next to reassuring yourself, the single most important thing you can do about your insurance program is to make sure you act like the commercial account that you are. For these purposes, divide the world of insurance agents into two kinds. One kind is composed of agents who sell mainly single automobile insurance, homeowners' insurance, etc., otherwise known as personal lines. The second kind is agents who specialize in insuring commercial enterprises of all sorts, and this is where you want to be. If you don't know what kind of insurance your existing agent specializes in, try what I call the Neon Sign Test. Go down to your agent's offices and look in the front window. If there are neon signs advertising "Auto Insurance Sold Here," think about getting another agent.

Why is it important that you choose a commercial lines agent? Because any nonprofit organization is ultimately a business, and you need an agent who is comfortable with the unique kind of risks a business entity poses. Your agent's familiarity with the insurance market is essential. The liability insurance industry historically lurches from boom to bust and back to boom again. During boom times insurance companies are more than ready to sell you insurance. During bust periods they pick their business extremely carefully and many nonprofit organizations have found themselves without insurance for no discernible reason. The cycles can come and go surprisingly fast, and you need an agent who can anticipate each one and represent you well under all conditions.

Your Insurance Agent Only Does Two Things

Your insurance agent is nothing more than an intermediary in the process of compiling the amount of financial protection your agency requires. As an intermediary, he or she has only two jobs. One is to "sell" you as a potential risk to an insurance company (marketing). The second is to see to it that all related administrative chores are taken care of once the sale is made (servicing). The first job is practically invisible to you as a customer except when the agent initially gathers the pertinent information to apply for insurance. Just as no two nonprofit organizations are exactly alike, neither are two insurance companies. Some companies like nonprofit "risks," others do not. Some that accept nonprofit business want only a certain size, or a certain kind. It is your agent's job to find a good match for your agency. That is what marketing means in this context.

Once your agency has purchased a policy, the agent's second job comes into focus. Even if you never submit a single claim on that insurance, you and your agent are likely to exchange correspondence or personal visits or both. Somewhere in the course of this process you will repeat your yearly vow never to speak with another insurance agent as long as you live. Resist the temptation. Careful attention to this phase can save you aggravation and perhaps even money later on. A good place to start is a careful reading of the policy itself. Details are critical here, so if you tend to break out in a cold sweat at the sight of an insurance policy (a colossal, soak-the-shoes cold sweat, not the normal shivers everyone gets), try to delegate that responsibility to a staff person, or—failing that—to a board member.

Why Your Insurance Agent Can't do Those Two Things Better

Unlike most of the other things your agency buys, insurance is an abstraction. You can't see it, taste it, feel it, or smell it. Keeping track of it isn't easy for anyone. Insurance agencies deal with the stuff every day, but they don't have foolproof systems for their businesses any more than nonprofit organizations have for theirs. Mistakes happen. For example, one unemployment insurance consultant I know swears that the absolute minimum error rate in processing claim forms is 10 percent. Once again, a good way to protect your operations from mistakes is to assign the responsibility for insurance matters to a single person or department.

Another thing you can do is to be sure that your insurance agency knows the way you handle insurance matters. If the insurance agency works with a lot of manufacturing firms it may be accustomed to dealing with full-time risk managers or other insurance professionals who know the lingo and whose job it is to deal with insurance affairs. Make the insurance agency understand that you do not have this type of resource, but ask as many questions as you need to in order to understand a particular type of coverage or charge.

Finally, make a point of learning how your particular demands deviate from the norm. Government funding imposed on a fund accounting system can produce some pretty tortured requests for information that the insurance agency may not routinely provide other customers. If your information request or change in procedures is valid and necessary, you are perfectly within your rights as a customer to demand it. But if you can simplify your request in any way you may save yourself one or more insurance headaches.

What You Can Do

As massive and complicated as this country's system of liability insurance may be, there are still many things that the individual nonprofit agency can do to improve the odds in its favor. What most of them have in common is that they start with new thinking.

Don't Assume the Law Will Protect You

Big Brother may be creeping into many parts of our society, but he has shown a complete lack of interest in overseeing the liability insurance world. I once met the former head of insurance for the federal government, an articulate fellow who had turned into a crusader for insurance consumers when he left office. I was duly impressed with his having served in what I assumed to be the center of enormous power to influence the insurance industry in this country. Then I learned that the federal head of insurance at that time oversaw a national program of flood insurance and urban burglary insurance. That was it. No rule-making capacity, no power to right consumer wrongs, no real authority to police any type of insurance offerings that didn't involve an excess of water or cat burglars.

Thanks to an obscure federal law passed in the late 1940s, the insurance industry in this country is regulated by exactly fifty people—the insurance commissioners of each state. When it comes to consumer protection, this is a mismatch on the order of King Kong versus Charlie Chaplin. In recent years there have been some stirrings in Congress about repealing the law, known as the McCarron-Ferguson Act, but repeal is a long distance away. Should it come, it would virtually guarantee massive changes in the way all businesses get their insurance—and the smart nonprofit executive will be positioned to take advantage of it.

For now, unless an individual state decides otherwise, there are no laws governing things that many consumers would consider the basics, such as how much insurance companies can charge or how quickly they can change their rates. Insurance companies do not have to tell you in advance that they are cancelling your insurance, nor must they tell you or anyone else how your collected premium stacked up against the claims paid on your behalf.

In practice, reputable insurance companies will do some of these things even if there is no law requiring them to. But they are doing so voluntarily, because the real aim of most government regulation of insurance companies is simply to make sure that the company is around to pay your claims if and when they occur. To that end, state governments impose all sorts of standards on the companies' fiscal health. But when it comes to the actual design-ing, selling, and servicing of insurance policies, you and the companies are on your own. The best protection you can get against potential insurance company capriciousness is a good insurance agent. How to select and work with an agent comes later on in this chapter.

Consider Hiring an Insurance Adviser

It may pay to hire expert advice. Your insurance agent can be a very good source of information, but even the most scrupulous and informed agent cannot always reconcile the demand to sell you insurance with your need to make economical use of your resources. True, insurance advisers never get a dime from selling insurance, but specialize instead in advising consumers on how to purchase it. Advisers can also be a diplomatic way of dealing with the long-time board member/insurance agent whose package you suspect is less than the best available.

How can you know whether it might pay to hire an adviser? There are no absolute guidelines, but liability insurance premiums in the five figures suggest a plan that might benefit from outside help. Try to get your insurance agent to pick up the cost of the consultation. And don't worry if your agency is located in a geographic area barren of insurance adviser types: a surprising amount can be accomplished over the telephone, via the mail, and through electronic communications.

Join an Association's Plan

Insurance is a natural service for associations of nonprofits to offer, and many have established effective programs for their members. In New Hampshire, for example, the Granite State Association for Human Services has begun offering member agencies an insurance program. The Connecticut Association for Rehabilitation Facilities has had insurance as a member service for several years, as have my own former association and countless others throughout the country. The advantage of an association plan is that it works like a cookie cutter: the same terms, conditions, and cost formulas for everyone in the group. This means that marketing and some administrative costs for the insurance agency are less and the resulting savings could be shared among all parties. It also means that when the insurance market goes bust and insurance is hard to get, the chances of association members being cancelled or nonrenewed are less than for agencies the insurance agent services as one account, if only because the insurance agency has the ability to make cancellation a bigger pain in the neck for the insurance company.

The disadvantages of association plans are that they are not necessarily cheaper, and that they cannot always serve the unusual risk. Especially as insurance companies become more sophisticated at gauging the amount of risk involved in a nonprofit organization's services, unusual programs and those perceived as high risk may have to go outside an association group to find the right coverage.

In this area of nonprofit management there is reason for optimism that better ways will be found soon. Since the liability insurance crises of the mid-1980s, a number of national and regional groups have taken an interest in finding more permanent solutions to the problems nonprofits have in protecting their operations. The main question is whether they will be able to devise programs that will take all comers, or have to resort to taking only the least risky of the risks. With many nonprofit agencies involved in perceived areas of high risk, such as AIDS treatment and routine medical care, it's a question of more than passing importance. The entrepreneurial nonprofit executive will be paying careful attention.

CHAPTER 12

(ALMOST) EVERYTHING YOU NEED TO KNOW ABOUT ACCOUNTING

STOP! Don't turn the page. I know what you're thinking. It goes something like this: Yuck. *Accounting is something done by short men with thick glasses who thought the worst part about fourth grade was summer vacation. Accounting is the thing that that one person or department in every organization is doing when your travel vouchers are questioned or you have to sign reimbursement slips in three different places. Accounting is what goes on immediately prior to any announcement of financial difficulties. In short, accounting is obscure, arbitrary, impersonal, complex, mysterious, burdensome, unnatural, bizarre, and perhaps of dubious intent.*

Maybe. Maybe not. In any event, the real point about accounting is that it is a reality of nonprofit management that every executive must cope with sooner or later, and that the entrepreneurial nonprofit executive knows how to turn to his or her advantage. But before you ride the beast it's better to know something about it.

First, let's talk about what accounting is *not*.

It's not rocket science. In 1982, according to the U.S. Bureau of Labor Statistics, there were 856,000 accountants employed in this country. If accounting is so difficult, why would 856,000 people have bothered with it? And if it were so complicated, how could your brother-in-law have learned it?

It's not bookkeeping. In some quarters accounting has to struggle to differentiate itself from the simpler job of recording raw transactions on which accounting decisions are based. Accounting

121

and bookkeeping are very closely allied, but they are still two separate types of business activities.

It's not police work. Accounting neither directly prevents fiscal wrongdoing nor deliberately tries to smoke it out once it's occurred. Think of accountants as intermediaries, either between the mountains of data that the corporation's business systems produce and the managers who need to make some sense out of it, or between the manager's reporting systems and the interested outsider.

It's not the language of business. This is a metaphor as reassuringly simple as it is misleading. To put it in human terms, accounting is more like a culture than it is a language. This is not to say that accounting does not have its own peculiar jargon—it does—just that its dominant purpose is to reinforce certain ways of thinking about and conveying ideas about money.

Next, a history lesson. Years ago, accountants talked about something they called "internal control" in a rather broad fashion. Listen to some accountantspeak from 1949:

> Internal control comprises the plan of organization and all of the coordinate methods and measures adopted within a business to safeguard its assets, check the accuracy and reliability of its accounting data, promote operational efficiency, and encourage adherence to prescribed managerial policies. This definition possibly is broader than the meaning sometimes attributed to the term. It recognizes that a 'system' of internal control extends beyond those matters which relate directly to the functions of the accounting and financial departments. Such a system might include budgetary control, standard costs, periodic operating reports, statistical analyses and the dissemination thereof, a training program designed to aid personnel in meeting their responsibilities, and an internal audit staff . . . [1]

Now, listen to these folks' successors thirty years later:

> The committee believes that an internal accounting control is one that is concerned with the reliability of financial statements and with the broad internal accounting control objectives of authorization, accounting, and asset safeguarding and, further, that account-

ing controls should extend to all external reports of historical financial information.[2]

Notice the shifted emphasis? Today, accountants are more concerned than ever with being able to say that the financial statements a corporation presents can be relied on by outsiders to present a fair picture of what is going on inside that corporation, financially speaking, at a given point in time. In this regard, nonprofits and publicly held corporations are similar, since the latter must present accurate information for use by the general investing public, while the nonprofit in some sense owes a public documentation of how it used the funds that society voluntarily gave up the right to tax.

Whatever happened to that broader stuff the 1949 accountants felt was within the accountant's legitimate range of attention? Well, "accounting" as it is commonly defined today has actually become a two-part field: financial accounting and management accounting. To oversimplify only a little bit, financial accounting is chiefly concerned with the financial inner workings of organizations for the purpose of reporting to outsiders, while management accounting is chiefly concerned with the financial inner workings of organizations for the purpose of helping managers to accomplish their mission.

It is probably obvious by now that financial accounting is the one that gets most of the attention and creates most of the anxiety. We'll deal with it first, then move on to management accounting in the next chapter.

Nine Principles for Better Accounting

You are not an accountant. Yet you need to know at least the basics of accounting in order to get the most out of your organization's financial resources. At the same time you have absolutely no desire to be bored silly by an extended introductory course in accounting. Let's compromise. Below is a list of nine principles of accounting. Memorize them.

Memorize?

Yes, memorize. You probably haven't memorized anything since high school, but here is something as close to a guarantee as you will find in any book: memorize and completely understand these nine principles of accounting and you will have mastered the foundation of what you as a nonaccountant will ever need to know about accounting.

Here they are.

1. *The principle of the entity.* Accounting is done for business entities, in our case for nonprofit corporations. It is also done for partnerships, for-profit corporations, government agencies, and just plain people. But in each case the accounting records are kept for a single, definable entity.

The other important point here for entrepreneurial nonprofit managers is that accounting energy should focus ultimately on the corporation as a whole, not just on individual projects or programs. You can't know what to do with any one tree if you don't know what the forest looks like.

2. *Money measurement.* Accounting deals only with things that can be measured in terms of money. Dedication, intensity, and commitment to the cause never appear on your balance sheet—the amount of money that people owe you does.

3. *The dual aspect nature of accounting.* Merchants were said to have invented the balance sheet hundreds of years ago, and it endures today. Simply put, the dual aspect nature of accounting means that an organization's assets, or things of value, must always equal the organization's liabilities plus its equities, or claims of ownership. Or, as a formula:

$$ASSETS = LIABILITIES + EQUITIES$$

To make some sense of this notion, remember the idea of the corporation as a separate, freestanding entity. Assets are those things of value that it owns as an entity. Liabilities and equities are claims on those assets that can be asserted at any time by entities outside of the organization, including other corporations and individuals. So a piece of real estate is an asset, while the unpaid portion of the mortgage used to purchase it is a liability that the bank has a right to claim.

Theoretically, if the organization shuts down and the assets are turned into cash for exactly the amount at which they are valued on the balance sheet, whatever remains after the liabilities have been satisfied are equities. In a profit-making organization those equities are called owner's equities, stockholders' earnings, and net worth. In nonprofits, the comparable figure is usually called something like "fund balance." The difference is that, while equities in a for-profit can be claimed by specific owners, a nonprofit's fund balance cannot be claimed by anyone except the authorizing level of government should the nonprofit go out of existence. This is truly the only inherent financial meaning of "nonprofit" that distinguishes it from for-profit forms of business.

4. *The going concern concept.* Accountants always assume that the entity will continue to exist indefinitely unless there is some evidence to the contrary. They do this not only because it's common sense, but because if an organization has definite plans for going out of existence, special rules apply for its accounting work.

5. *The cost concept.* Whenever an organization buys something substantial, like a building or some land, that asset is listed at its cost. Here is another instance where the market value of an asset has nothing to do with the way it is listed in financial statements. Why concentrate on cost and ignore market value? For one thing, market values can change rapidly and dramatically. For another, "market value" in one observer's mind may be far different from another's, and there is no ready-made way of deciding between the two. The purchase price, however, is indisputable. Also, if the organization is planning to hold onto the asset and use it—echoes of the going concern concept here—who cares what the market value is anyway?

6. *Conservatism.* Accountants deliberately take the most cautious approach possible by accepting as real any decreases in equity (rough translation: expenses) as soon as they are reasonably possible, while accepting increases in equity (rough translation: revenues) only when they are reasonably certain. Another way to explain it: acknowledge bad news when you hear about it on the phone, good news only when it's in writing.

7. *Materiality.* Most people think of accountants as people ob-

sessed with trivialities, an image reinforced by the unfortunate term "bean counters." But good accounting deals only with matters having some significance in the overall scheme of things.

Many funding sources, especially government agencies, could use a refresher course in this part of accounting. In the name of accountability, they often demand elegantly minute explanations of how each and every dollar was spent, utterly disregarding the bigger picture. I once spent the better part of an hour arguing with a government accountant over whether a bill for $1.47 for ice cream cones submitted by one of my group homes for the mentally retarded was an expense for food or recreation. Ordinarily, details of that sort wouldn't interest me any more than they would interest you, but at stake was whether the five thousand dollar invoice of which the $1.47 was a part was to be paid in two days or two weeks.

The materiality concept really cuts two ways. It allows you to disregard the trivial, but it also means that you must disclose the important. In financial terms the place where the greatest number of important details are voluntarily disclosed is the footnotes to the financial statements. The footnotes are usually a rich source of in-depth information about the reporting organization and are worth wading through.

8. *Realization concept.* Whenever an organization delivers a service, it is entitled to say that it is owed some money for that service. Whether it actually gets the money or not is an entirely different matter, but for the moment let's assume that we haven't reached that point yet. If the organization delivers the service and has to wait to get paid, it establishes something called an account receivable. Accounts receivable are considered an asset of the organization, and it is reasonable to assume that all or most of the accounts receivable will be turned into cash sooner or later.

Accounts receivable for many nonprofit organizations are a hidden gold mine waiting to be tapped with the right skills and administrative commitment. Most of the groups I have worked with do a significant amount of business with government, and, predictably, the government agencies usually owe them a hefty amount of cash at any one time. I am constantly amazed at how a determined executive can cut down on the average amount of time it takes to collect outstanding receivables and change a good portion of them into cash in the bank. Most of the time all it takes is a consistent emphasis on keeping accounts receivable—which are essentially interest-free loans—to a minimum. The same principle applies to nonprofits supported through memberships and sustained giving drives. More on these areas later.

9. *Matching concept.* One of the simplest concepts, yet one of the easiest to lose sight of in the real world, is the idea that costs associated with the revenues in any given accounting period are expenses of that period. The wise manager will know that, from time to time, there will be a temptation to postpone recognizing certain costs as expenses, but that, over time, the consistency of the matching concept is a powerful force.

Setting Up Your Accounting System

You should keep two things in mind when you set up your accounting system, or review a system already in place. The first is so routine by now that it barely deserves mention, but we'll do it for the record: be sure to use the accrual method of accounting. The alternative to accrual accounting is cash accounting, which is what you and I do for our personal finances. Running a household solely on the basis of what goes in and out of the checkbook without any periodic summaries or attention paid to changes in equity is fine, but nonprofit organizations need more accountability and predictability than cash accounting can provide.

Fortunately, the vast majority of nonprofit organizations use accrual accounting now, so this should not be much of a problem. It can be complicated and will take more work on everyone's part, but the benefits are many times greater than the costs.

On the other hand, the benefits of another tenet of nonprofit accounting theory are not nearly so clear-cut. In any extended discussion of nonprofit financial matters, the idea of fund accounting is sure to be raised. Fund accounting is a system of accounting for financial performance according to the sources of the funds raised. Professor Robert Anthony of Harvard University tells of an extreme case of fund accounting in the U.S. Postal Service which at one time was said to have had one fund for first-class mail, another for third-class, another for money orders, and so on.[3] Furthermore, each individual post office was expected to maintain a *separate bank account* for each fund. Can there be any doubt that all hope for true accountability was obliterated by such a literal interpretation of the concept?

The first clue about the desirability of fund accounting for the entrepreneurial nonprofit executive comes from the number of for-profit companies that use fund accounting for their own operations: zero. In for-profit groups, all the resources coming into the organization are considered to be part of the same "pot" and can be treated accordingly, whereas the logical effect of fund accounting in a nonprofit is to break the corporation down into as many different separate entities as there are funds.

To be fair, things go on in the financial life of a nonprofit that have no counterpart in the for-profit sector. Only nonprofits, for example, get capital contributions, and often they need to be able to track those contributions right through the organization. Still, although it may be desirable for purposes of internal control to be able to separate out operations in this fashion, there are other ways of accomplishing the same thing without the inherent disadvantages of a fund accounting system.

The real damage that fund accounting can do to the unwitting executive, however, is psychological, not administrative. Think about the double-barreled implication in a system of accounting driven by a pervasive need to document the sources and uses of funds. Number one, it virtually says that the donor thinks there is a good chance that the funds will be used against his or her express wishes. Number two, it forces the nonprofit executive to be more concerned with keeping track of how money is spent than with whether the mission is being accomplished.

Some will argue that donors have a right to know that their donations are being handled properly and effectively. No argument there. But if one does not trust the recipient organization to use donations well, and in any case does not support the organization's overall mission, why donate at all?

How to Talk to Your CPA

Occasionally one encounters a social mechanism that is brilliantly conceived and, from society's point of view, stunningly well executed. Such is the case with the American system of certified public accountants.

Consider this. If I were to climb up on a soapbox in my local park and propose that the government mount an army of accountants, all with specialized training and demonstrated allegiance to the pronouncements of a centralized authority, to go into the offices of every publicly held company and most nonprofit agencies for the purpose of assuring the citizenry that the public interest was duly protected during the course of a year's worth of business, I would be politely ignored as just another eccentric in a tattered sweater.

Of course, except for the fact that this particular army is rightfully called a profession and that it is paid for entirely by the groups being investigated rather than the government, this is precisely what public accounting is all about.

Skeptical? Look at it this way. The most important products produced for an organization by a CPA firm are the yearly financial statements. But virtually everything in the yearly financial statements can and should have been produced periodically during the previous year by staff or consultants of the corporation being audited. The only thing in the financial statements that could not be done by the corporation's staff, in fact, is a single sheet of paper—the auditors' letter to the board of directors.

A sample auditors' letter is included here.

The Board of Directors
Anycorp, Inc.
Happyville, USA

We have examined the balance of Anycorp, Inc., at June 30, 1990, and the related statements of support and revenue, expenses and capital additions, changes in fund balances, functional expenses, and changes in financial position for the year then ended. Our examination was made in accordance with generally accepted auditing standards, and accordingly included such tests of the accounting records and such other auditing procedures as we considered necessary in the circumstances.

In our opinion, the aforementioned financial statements present fairly the financial position of Anycorp, Inc., at June 30, 1990, and the results of its operations and the changes in its fund balances and financial position for the year then ended, in conformity with generally accepted accounting principles applied on a consistent basis.

The totals for 1989, presented for comparative purposes only, were taken from financial statements for the year ended June 30, 1989, which were examined by us, and we expressed an unqualified opinion on them in our report dated September 1, 1989.

Probit and Billim
Certified Public Accountants

September 1, 1990

In the end, it is that second paragraph for which the nonprofit organization pays a CPA firm anywhere from a few thousand to a few hundred thousand dollars—"In our opinion the aforementioned financial statements present fairly the financial position. . . ." At an audit fee of, say, five thousand dollars, that's a thousand dollars per line, $94.34 per word, $17.86 per letter. Not a bad price for reassurance to anyone who might be listening that accounting professionals have reviewed your books and think that you're presenting a pretty honest picture of what is really going on financially with your corporation.

Notice that there are a few reassurances missing. For example, "These people polish every dime before they spend it so you can feel safe giving them money." Or, "We looked under every rock in the joint and couldn't find a single crook." Nor is there any suggestion that the organization is free of waste, fraud, abuse, incompetence, or inefficiency. All of those things could in fact be going on undetected in the corporation no matter what the CPA letter says because CPAs are not intended, nor do they want, to be the Financial Police. All they are there to do is exactly what they say in their letter—examine the books to decide if they paint an accurate portrait of the organization's finances.

Picking Your CPA

Inevitably the question arises, "Should we hire a big-name accounting firm to do our books?" Usually the query is good for at least a few minutes of heated discussion at the board level, regardless of whether the agency is using a well-known accounting firm to prepare its audited financial statements or not. It's the wrong question.

Public accounting is changing rapidly. It used to be that there were a handful of major national accounting firms—the Big Eight—and then everyone else. Now, after mergers in the latter part of the '80s, the Big Eight has become the Big Six, and many regional accounting firms have moved to expand their own scope. There are many good reasons for hiring one of the big accounting firms, but trying to avoid a risk by choosing an ostensibly known commodity is not one of them.

Instead of asking whether the agency should hire a big-name firm, decision makers need to ask, "What is it that we need a CPA firm to do?" Then, consider the answers along three separate dimensions.

Size. Using only size as a criterion makes the decision easy. Small nonprofit organizations normally cannot afford much more than rock-bottom accounting services and prices to match. This tends to push them in the direction of small, local outfits. Conversely, larger institutions for whom the yearly audit is a matter of pulling together massive amounts of data from innumerable departments into a coherent whole need the services of a similarly broad accounting firm with lots of manpower to put on the job. In this case one of the large national firms is often a practical choice.

Another less obvious factor makes the choice easy. Accounting firms are service organizations whose product is deeply rooted in the qualifications of the people working for the firm. David Maister has described the well-known accounting firms as hierarchies composed of three distinct types of professionals: finders, minders, and grinders.[4]

In this view, grinders are the people on the front lines—the young men and women in new suits purchased especially for the job who show up at your office for a few days or a few weeks and actually pore over the books making notes and doing hundreds of calculations.

Minders, on the other hand, are the folks who used to be grinders. They've made it to the next level of the company, and their responsibilities are essentially those of middle managers. They too have new suits, but a better grade.

At the top are the finders, or partners. These are the actual owners of the firm, having gotten that way by passing through the grinder and minder stages with enough momentum to convince other partners that they were the sort of people it would be nice to have around for a lifetime.

Competition for partner slots is genteel but brutal. By some accounts, fewer than 5 percent of any one crop of grinders will survive to become finders. Promotions must come at regular intervals or the message to locate other employment is clear. New recruits generally know the unwritten expectations when they come in and expect the experience to pay off in later jobs anyway, so the game is understood by everyone.[5]

I saw how it worked when I used a Big Eight firm. One year, the grinder would show up ready to perform his or her first nonprofit audit. The next year, he or she would be a minder, and we would get a new grinder, and so on. Under those circumstances, it isn't hard to figure out which grinders are going to be assigned to the account of a small nonprofit organization.

Of course, this dynamic can actually benefit the small nonprofit should the grinder turn out to be someone with a sincere interest in nonprofit accounting and enough personal security not to be threatened by the prospect of being perceived to have stepped off the upward track. But on the whole, small nonprofits and large CPA firms are not the most efficient match.

Complexity. Were size the only standard by which to measure the organization's need for CPA services, the choices would be a lot less ambiguous. But the entrepreneurial nonprofit manager knows that the complexity of the organization, especially in today's world of increasingly sophisticated nonprofit financing and organizational structure, is a second important element to keep in mind when selecting an auditing firm.

Taxes are a prime area in which the nonprofit organization might benefit from the in-house expertise a large accounting firm can offer. Unrelated business income taxes, excess lobbying excise tax, real estate taxes, and various types of payments in lieu of taxes are some of the now routine complications nonprofits may face. As with any intelligent outside advice, a seemingly high out-of-pocket cost for some timely wisdom can actually save many thousands of dollars later on.

Many nonprofits, especially those in the health and human service world, are taking a page from the corporate book and organizing operations as subsidiaries of larger holding companies. Often, one or more of these subsidiaries is a proprietary enterprise. Another type of complexity results when nonprofits cross state or international lines, increasingly a reality for services like adoption or specialized human services. All of these situations demand a level of sensitivity and technical expertise beyond what the local firm may be able to offer, particularly since the CPA needs to act as much like a management consultant as an auditor in these exotic realms of financial accountability.

Visibility. The third and final standard for assessing your organization's needs for auditing services is something of a trump card. Small or large, simple or complex, if a nonprofit organization's mission brings with it a lot of visibility, there may be no substitute for the implied name-brand endorsement of a national auditing firm.

The theory here, of course, is that the national outfit has more to lose if it wrongly approves a set of financial statements that later turn out to have been hugely and perhaps criminally wrong. In actuality, it's the smallish local firm that stands to be hurt the most if that happens, since it will have neither the resources nor the reputation to survive a prolonged period of public mistrust.

Be careful not to jump to conclusions about just how visible your organization really is. And don't let others jump either. There is an understandable tendency to equate a firm's size and stature with quality of service, and to assume that a well-known name means superior service. Focus instead on the fit between your organization's needs and your auditor's resources in order to insure the best opportunity for both parties.

CHAPTER 13

THE FIVE FINANCIAL REPORTS YOU NEED

If you need to control a nonprofit organization and deep in your heart you know you are one of those people for whom data is the plural of anecdote, this chapter is for you.

When the history of Western civilization in the twentieth century is written, the characteristic that will cause the greatest amount of headshaking among our historian descendants will be our degree of information pollution. With fascination and no small degree of amusement, they will look at our century-long love affair with the idea of management and marvel at how we were able to create such a series of ever faster and more powerful systems for keeping track of too much of the wrong information.

If you run a nonprofit organization and would like to establish a reasonable management information and financial control system, you have the chance to strike your own small blow against the scourge of information overload. Your contribution to this effort is to ask for exactly five reports on a regular basis: balance sheet, income and expense report, aged receivables, cash flow projections, and service utilization.

We'll go into what you do with those reports a bit later. First, let's talk about the glue that holds them together. It's called accountability. Accountability is one of those words that recently has become so larded with negative meaning that it only seems to call up images of overpriced Pentagon screwdrivers. Still, accountability is what you need. All it means is that you have a built-in structure for using every morsel of information that your management control systems faithfully generate.

One helpful way of thinking about management control information is what I call the Lost Sleep test: *Every material piece of information in your five financial reports should cause one senior manager to lose sleep if it fails to live up to pre-determined expectations.* Allow for psychobiological differences, of course; headaches, tearfulness, nail-biting, upset stomachs, and the like can be substituted for lost sleep. The point is to create ownership of outcomes, and to design a control system that supports it.

The secondary point is that in matters of nonprofit management control less is more. Better to have fewer reports that produce a high degree of information that actually gets used than more reports, each of which manages to present one or two interesting facts. My personal, unproven feeling is that no normal human being ever consistently looks at more than three reports on a regular basis, so five is admittedly pushing it. Fortunately, most of these five reports can be broken up for use by a number of different people, so few people have to absorb all five (sorry, but you're probably one of them).

One last thought on the whole notion of management control. The word itself promises more than can be delivered, as though management control were as mechanistic a matter as the steering system in a car—turning the steering wheel x inches equals y degrees of turning radius in the front wheels. It's not nearly that simple. By the time any event takes its place in one of your reports as a number, there is virtually no hope of controlling it. The idea is for any one of the basic five reports to offer a look backward in time that gives some insight about the future. That's where management can have its impact, though usually more in the way of shaping than controlling.

Here are the reports, along with some suggestions for how to use them.

1. Balance Sheet

In addition to being the anchor report of a traditional group of financial statements, the balance sheet can also be a valuable tool for management control. Essentially just a compilation of the things of value that an organization owns set off against outsiders' claims and "equities," the balance sheet in many ways is the organization's monthly report card. You can use it as an implicit check on your management control structure by holding one person ultimately accountable for each line item.

To see how this works, dig out your most recent tax return (IRS form 990) and follow along.

Assets

Cash and Cash Investments. In a nonprofit corporation, cash is king. No shareholders are going to storm your annual meeting because you didn't pay out dividends; suppliers are likely to hear "nonprofit" and automatically assume you'll have trouble paying your bills; and the IRS may even be a trifle less inclined to play hardball with back taxes. But when you run out of cash, you've run out of gas. Cash is so important that it deserves its own special report, detailed below. Assign this one to your highest ranking business type and check below for what to ask.

Accounts Receivable. Second to cash in importance is the amount of money outsiders owe you that you have yet to collect. Accounts receivable also merit a separate report as detailed below, and a full-time business-type person assigned to them if the volume justifies it. To get an idea of how well you are performing right now, calculate this ratio:

$$\text{Total Accounts Receivable} \div \text{Total All Assets}$$

If this formula works out to, say, 33 percent or less, you may have a financially sound organization. On the other hand, anything over 50 percent should tell you that your flexibility is severely limited. And if you register over 75 percent, especially if the bulk of the funds receivable are with only one or two funding sources, you don't own the receivables, *they own you.*

The next thing you need to find out is how your ratio compares to others'. The percentage of assets carried in the form of receivables will vary according to the type of service you provide, the complexity and sophistication of your agency and funding source, and even the time of year. This is true of every industry, because the economics are unique to specific types of corporations. Grocery stores, for example, will have almost no receivables since their business is largely cash or easily cashed checks. At the other extreme are professional service firms, which can carry receivables for as long as five months or more before they're paid.

Think about this ratio as an index of how nice you are. A large amount of receivables means you are so nice that you let outside parties—your clients or funding sources—hang onto a large chunk of your agency. Your ability to get access to cash at a moment's notice is diminished, you have less money available for investment, and you are effectively at the mercy of the payment policies of whomever owes you the money. Do you really want to be that nice?

Pledges and Grants Receivable. These are exactly like accounts receivable except for the obvious difference that they come from philanthropic sources. Whoever writes the grant proposals and oversees the fund-raising campaign gets to worry about this line. In small organizations this will usually be the executive director, in larger ones the director of development. The responsibility is a bit tricky, since zero pledges and grants receivable may mean that the agency's fund-raising effort is lax, or it could mean that it is uncommonly efficient in collecting donations before allowing them to even become pledges. The time of the year will also affect this line—an end of the fiscal year fund-raising campaign will produce lots more volume here than at most other times of the year.

This is one area to which the entrepreneurial nonprofit manager will pay careful attention in the coming years because standards for handling pledges receivable looked like they were about to change as this book was being written. The Financial Accounting Standards Board (FASB) planned to announce a proposed new policy requiring nonprofit corporations to show pledges as receivable, something most organizations are reluctant to do in order to avoid the kind of experience Princeton University had a few years ago.

A wealthy and well-known businessman told the university that he would donate it $1.5 million. As was their policy, Princeton officials kept the pledge off their balance sheet as an asset, preferring to wait until the money was actually received. This turned out to be a wise decision, for the businessman was Ivan Boesky, and before he could make good on his pledge he was indicted on insider trading charges and suddenly had much more pressing demands on his personal fortune. Pay attention to the opportunities in this accounting change.

Inventories. Under ordinary circumstances, inventories are a nonissue for most nonprofits. If you have any substantial amount, however, this line is the report card for the person ultimately responsible for using them.

Investments and Securities. Don't try to play where you don't belong. Any substantial amount of investments and securities calls for professional management. When you hire an adviser you'll get more regular detailed reports than would appear on your balance sheet, so by the time you see this number it shouldn't be a surprise.

Land, Buildings and, Equipment. In truth, this line may be difficult to use for internal control purposes because it will incorporate such diverse assets as your office building and your shiny new computer system. Still, let it serve as a reminder that tangible assets need routine maintenance and repair prescribed and arranged by some responsible party.

Other Assets. Your other assets will vary from zero to a substantial amount, depending on the nature of the organization. Art museums, for example, will ordinarily carry a large percentage of their assets here. In that case, it's the curator's scorecard.

Liabilities

Accounts Payable and Accrued Expenses. You can benefit from assigning two-level responsibility here. The operational level demands a clerical/bookkeeper-type who can do a repetitive job accurately (consider having identical recurring expenses paid automatically—lease payments, for example). Then be sure that the highest ranking financial type—or you—routinely reviews scheduled payments. In tough times you may be able to stretch some of the nonpersonnel payments, and in good times you only need to be sure to pay bills on time (earlier if you get a discount). Good bill paying is a balancing act and demands constant attention.

Mortgages and Other Notes Payable. Now we get into top leadership territory. This line measures your agency's degree of long-term indebtedness. If you would like to know how far into hock you've gone, take this number, add it to any other line showing debt that must be paid off for more than a twelve-month period, and divide it by your total unrestricted fund balance. This will give you an approximation of the relationship between your credit commitments and your agency's ability to pay them off. As with most ratios, there is no absolute standard against which to judge individual performance, but any result approaching or exceeding 1.0 could mean lessened ability to handle additional debt. In turn, this implies that growth will have to be financed through yearly operations, not borrowing, and that your overall ability to maneuver through a fiscal crisis could be limited.

Fund Balances. Deep in the heart of leadership country we find this euphemism for net worth. Simplistically, it's what could be expected to be left over for the outside world to claim were all of the agency's assets to be used at listed values to satisfy all liabilities (i.e., claims by outsiders). Ordinarily the place where for-profit corporations show owners' and/or stockholders' equity, a nonprofit's fund balance is really "owned" by the public since it can have no shareholders in the legal sense of the term. If the entrepreneurial nonprofit executive has a report card, this line is it. Good program performance and a steadily growing fund balance are the twin peaks of agency achievement.

2. Profit and Loss Statement

Let's be forthright and call this one a profit and loss statement even though the more up-to-date terms are operating statement or statement of revenue and expenses. After all, ultimately the only number of importance in this report is the one telling you whether the agency made a profit for the month or lost money. Don't make this any more complicated than it needs to be.

As with the balance sheet, however, since this statement is part of a good accounting system's monthly output anyway, you ought to put it to use in your management control system. To do so you simply need to parse out responsibility for various elements of the overall profit and loss picture. Start by dividing the organization into Lost Sleep Centers—definable organizational locations occupied by a single person having clear-cut responsibility for all that goes on beneath him or her. Staff occupying a Lost Sleep Center simply need to be responsible for *something*. Often what they are responsible for is as simple as all the real property owned by the agency. Or the computer system. Or a social work department. In these cases, the segment does not produce revenue, so the real focus is on controlling expenses.

More often the Lost Sleep Center (LSC) person should be responsible for generating a profit from his or her operations. Keeping track of this profit gives you a two-level control system: agency-wide and program-specific, as shown below:

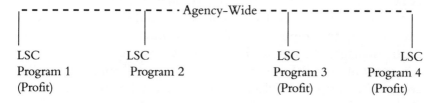

Together, all profits or losses, plus the costs managed by Lost Sleep Centers without profit responsibilities, should add up to the agency-wide profit (or loss). The benefit of this system is that it allows agency-wide responsibilities to be broken down into more manageable chunks and assigned to specific individuals, along with comparable delegations of authority.

A critical second step is to set up the ability to compare budgeted revenues and expenses with actual amounts every month. Some advise comparing revenues and expenses with last year's revenues and expenses, and while this may be an interesting exercise in institutional history it's largely a waste of time. The point of an internal control system is to exercise some executive authority, and one does that by shaping the future, not fretting about the past. Imperfect as it usually is, the best financial tool we have for shaping the future is the budget that we projected that future would require. Use it, compare it with actual results, and be sure to understand the reasons for variances.

Having set up an internal control system based in part on the profit and loss statement, the next step is to back off. For ninety days. Monthly blips up or down occur too frequently in most agencies to take them seriously until there is a trend. Reviewing actual versus budgeted performance with those in charge of all Lost Sleep Centers every three months gives a chance for trends and patterns to develop while still leaving enough time to correct problems. (For more on the general topic of using budgets entrepreneurially, see Chapter 14, Budgeting for Success.)

3. Cash Flow Projections

Now we arrive at the reports not ordinarily part of a standard financial accounting package. This one should be. It is hard to overestimate the importance of cash to the entrepreneurial nonprofit manager. In for-profit entities, it's usually outsiders with some sort of financial stake in the organization—banks, shareholders, owners, etc.—who decide whether and when to fold up and go home. Because nonprofits have no possibility of ownership, and have perhaps more leeway from bankers and suppliers, the impetus to shut them down is more likely to come from within, and the most inescapable way that that happens is when the agency simply runs out of cash. Put positively, the surest way to stick around as a nonprofit is to have enough cash at all times.

The cash flow report should be as much a part of your regular control system as the first two reports. It starts with a cash flow budget for the coming year. For the agency as a whole, the first step is to associate the cash inflow for each month for each type of revenue, then do the same for each type of expense. Computerized spreadsheets make it easier to do this, but in all honesty the chief requirement for doing it correctly is the ability to tolerate a heavy dose of tediousness. Estimating the amount of cash received for each month and the amount paid out for each kind of expense takes persistence, thoughtfulness, and a speck of imagination. Unfortunately, a cash flow projection put together without benefit of all these qualities hovers dangerously close to being useless.

Once you have a projection for the year (consider turning it into a graph for those uncomfortable with seeing endless columns of numbers), take a moment to ponder the implications. I once managed an association heavily dependent on member dues, which came in during the period from December to February. The real problem with this pattern was that it was extremely hard even for the experienced among us to keep from getting positively giddy each winter when we had stored up cash equal to eight or nine months' expenses. It took constant training and reminders to ourselves that we'd be one hungry pack of squirrels if we didn't leave some of those acorns for the following November.

Next, apply the exact same comparative structure that you did with your budgets: show where you expected to be each month versus where you actually are. The only differences are that for expenses it's acceptable to use a single number showing the amount of cash spent during that period, and that you also need to account for cash outflows released for the purpose of acquiring assets.

How often you revisit your cash flow projection will depend on how volatile your cash flow is. The more stable the flow, the less frequently projections need to be redone. Generally, quarterly reprojections should be sufficient except in periods of predicted volatility, when monthly or bimonthly would be advisable.

4. Aged Receivables Report

Finally, a report you may never have considered could be the key to organizational health and good fortune—or at least to a better cash flow. Any nonprofit corporation that provides a service for payment at some point in the future by definition has accounts receivable, and the entrepreneurial nonprofit manager knows that accounts receivable can be a fiscal gold mine easily tapped.

To get some idea of how rapidly you are collecting the money owed to you right now, calculate two simple ratios. First, figure out how much revenue you need to receive every day of the year on average. Do this by dividing last year's total revenue by the 365 days in a year. This ratio gives you one day's worth of revenue.

Next, locate the line for total accounts receivable on last year's audited balance sheet. This figure tells you how much money was yet to be received for services rendered as of the last day of the fiscal year, presumably a representative amount. Divide this number by one day's worth of revenue and check the result. You have just calculated your agency's collection period, or the average number of days it takes to collect on a bill.

By itself, the collection period will tell you little, although it helps to ask yourself whether the amount of time it takes you to collect seems right for your environment. Generally, the larger the bills or the more complicated the billing mechanism, the longer the collection period. You get the most value from knowing your collection period by comparing it to similar organizations' ratios. Associations of nonprofits are a good source for this kind of information, and occasionally business-oriented publications contain it as well.

If there is a secret in the collection business, it's knowing how old each of your uncollected bills is. Naturally, the longer a bill is outstanding, the less chance there is of it being paid. So each month you need a report showing which receivables are outstanding for thirty days or less, which for sixty, which for ninety, and which for more than ninety. A little attention to economics will help you focus on the younger bills that have a greater chance of getting paid than the dusty old ones that have been sitting around for a few months. Of course, the older bills need attention too, just the more concentrated and expensive kind. All the more reason to keep bills from growing old before their time.

What can you do? Entrepreneurial nonprofit executives understand that creative solutions to collection problems are available, often with low price tags and high paybacks. The simplest thing to do is the cheapest and frequently the most potent: state firmly and often that rapid bill collection is important. That ought to be good for, say, a 10 percent improvement in collection period. If that translated into a 10 percent improvement in cash balances, it would mean something like a one-half to one percent improvement in interest earned or an equivalent reduction in interest paid on a cash flow loan.

Timely telephone calls bringing gentle reminders can be effective also. Again, the improvement may only be to get the bill paid two days earlier than it would have been paid otherwise, but this is a game where the little pieces add up. Where payments from third parties are routine, some mental and other health agencies assign staff to make sure that prospective patients are fully aware of all their legitimate claims on third-party payments, and that those claims are properly processed.

More expensive but potentially high payback methods of improving receivables collection performance include hiring additional staff, investing in computer upgrading, and expanding basic capacities such as telephone systems.

5. Utilization Report

An indispensable tool for the entrepreneurial nonprofit manager is some form of utilization reporting system. Ideally, it will be linked to the financial accounting system and will generate invoices, make tracking revenue sources easier, and help manage receivables. Designed properly, a utilization reporting system will also generate a respectable database for use in future marketing efforts.

Unlike the previous four reports, the utilization report must be tailored specifically to an individual agency and its array of services. No off-the-shelf products here, although a computerized spreadsheet could be very helpful. As with the profit and loss and cash flow projection, the idea is to compare actual results with projected outcomes, and, more important, to understand the reasons for every major deviance.

While service utilization reporting is especially important for nonprofits that depend on fees and service-based income, all should have some means of documenting levels of service utilization, if only to be able to prove the demand for their services should the occasion ever arise. The entrepreneurial nonprofit manager puts a system in place well before it's ever needed.

Internal Financial Controls

Read enough audit reports and management letters to nonprofit organizations from public agencies or their own accounting firms and you'll notice that the most frequently cited area of concern is weak internal controls. What this means is that inherent in the groups' own processes are opportunities for fraud, duplication of activities, and inadequate control over fiscal resources. It does *not* mean that any of these things actually occurs, and in fact the fiduciary aspect of the nonprofit executive's job may actually attract more than its share of people disinclined to perpetrate fraud in the workplace.

Considering the aspect of public trust embedded in the nonprofit manager's job, it's a fair question to ask why such a basic matter as adequate internal controls is nevertheless so frequently overlooked. It used to be that one could point to the lack of interest and/or sophistication in financial matters on the part of nonprofits to explain this kind of thing, but I think the real reason was and is much more mundane: lack of administrative staff.

Built into the idea of internal controls is a premise so fundamental that it's easy to overlook. *To establish a traditional system of internal financial controls requires spreading duties among several people.* When a nonprofit organization gets along with a volunteer president, an executive director, a part-time bookkeeper who tries to double as a business manager, and a single clerk, there is not a lot of spreading that can happen. It's not that the average nonprofit manager doesn't want an adequate system of internal financial controls, it's just that the resources don't seem to be there.

Fortunately, there is something most organizations can do. With a little careful organizing and judicious use of staff time, even the smallest of nonprofits can mount a credible set of internal controls.

CHAPTER 14

BUDGETING FOR SUCCESS

Revoke my MBA for saying it, but budgeting for a nonprofit organization has very little to do with rows of tiny little numbers on a sheet of paper. By the time things get to that stage, it's largely a job for smart technicians and good computers, preferably at least one of each. The executive's work takes place long before, and regardless of the size or nature of the organization it consists almost exclusively of wrestling with three permanent, inescapable tensions: the demand for services versus available revenue, the old versus the new, and direct program costs versus administration.

Humpty Was onto Something

If there is one thing about tax-exempt organizations that every donor, every Community Chest volunteer, every recipient of service, every professional athlete cum fund-raiser, every government official, and a good many employees of nonprofit corporations themselves certainly know, it is that administration is a dirty word.

Administration is the place where unaccountable, morally suspect things happen. As a unique creature inside the nonprofit, administration is always too large, and it invariably has a voracious appetite for more money. Despite its size, administration rarely tries to do anything on behalf of the organization, and the few things it tries to do it does wrong. If administration were to go

147

out of existence no one would miss it, and the programs might finally get what they needed.

I know whereof I speak. I came into my first nonprofit administration job harboring similar sentiments, which were obliterated after about three days when I realized that my treasured program goals were never going to get accomplished without some rock solid administration behind them. I spent the rest of my tenure trying to figure out how to reconcile the two conflicting points of view.

Too bad no one told me it was impossible. Too bad no one told me not to waste my time trying. The problem isn't so much that neither side knows when to stop arguing—although that is definitely *part* of the problem—but that neither side knows how to talk to the other. They have no common ground of agreement, no common language even, and usually neither side knows it. The result is endless tension and fruitless organizational bickering. It's worse when the antiadministration forces are from outside the organization, ten times worse when they happen to represent funding sources.

Two principles that all parties ought to be able to agree upon are that administrative costs should be kept to the most efficient minimum possible and that the purpose of administration in any nonprofit organization is to help program people advance the mission-related goals. The last point is particularly important. It needs to be communicated constantly and sincerely by all administrative types that their presence is secondary to program, that their role is to enable and empower the people actually carrying out the group's mission.

If administration representatives actually perform this role, it will go a long way toward diminishing the ambivalence toward them by program personnel. Unfortunately, it does little for outsiders with the same ambivalence. For a clue as to how to handle them, we turn to the looking glass:

> "But 'glory' doesn't mean 'a nice knockdown argument,' " Alice objected.
>
> "When *I* use a word," Humpty Dumpty said, in rather a scornful tone, "it means just what I choose it to mean—neither more nor less."

"The question is," said Alice, "whether you *can* make words mean so many different things."

"The question is," said Humpty Dumpty, "which is to be master—that's all."

Lewis Carroll, *Through the Looking Glass*

Administrative costs are a fiction, an abstract concept called into existence because practicality can't keep up with the elegance of the human brain. Administrative costs—or, more accurately, indirect costs—are indirect only because it is neither practical nor desirable to create and maintain systems that will keep track of every last paper clip and every ten-minute chunk of an executive director's time in order to say with confidence that those resources were spent on behalf of agency program A rather than agency program B. As a compromise, budgeters lump all such indirect costs together and figure out an equitable way of charging them against each of the agency's programs.

Exactly how big that lump is and what it comprises will vary according to a wide variety of factors. The central point is that it's all a matter of definition, and why not tailor the agency's definition of "administrative costs" so as to best preserve the sensibilities of those funding it?

One executive director I know carried this idea to an extreme. The annual report of his four-million-dollar day-care agency carefully demonstrated that the organization spent only $160,000 on overhead costs. Considering that the group ran ten day-care centers scattered over a thirty-mile radius, owned a first-rate computer system, paid competitive administrative salaries, and had its headquarters in the middle of one of the country's most expensive cities, this number was as miraculous as it was preposterous. But in displaying it he communicated an implicit oath to the reader that administration deserved to be kept to a minimum, and that potential donations would be used efficiently.

The only problem with this solution—other than the fact that the agency needs to be scrupulously careful not to abuse it—is that all top management needs to understand and carefully monitor the bulk of the overhead costs being charged directly to programs in order to keep tight control.

Old Versus New

This budgetary tension of old programs versus new ones is immeasurably complicated by outside factors over which the executive has little or no influence. Many of these factors are predisposed toward new efforts. For example, in an earlier chapter I covered the bias toward the new inherent in most foundation funding. It also happens to be easier to motivate staff and board to pour energy into building the new than maintaining the old. Most government funding or regulatory systems tend to use a reimbursement structure geared to historical costs in one way or another that have the effect of rewarding the new while cementing funding inequities in old programs.

Yet any nonprofit organization needs a solid base of existing programs to operate while exploring new directions, and the budget is where the balance between these competing interests must be struck. The executive's role here is twofold: keep up the old programs while pushing them forward in new ways.

At the heart of this balancing act is the organization's style of changing itself, and what makes this aspect of nonprofit management so challenging is the frequent lack of widely accepted performance standards. If you and I both work for a nonprofit organization, and there are no generally accepted standards of success for our agency's activities, then your guess is as good as mine about whether the organization should be changing and, if so, in what way. If you and I disagree and there is no strong third party to referee, the only way for one of us to win is for the other to get tired of the fight or leave the agency.

Once a certain program model or way of doing things has passed from new to old, the tendency of funding sources, staff, and program users alike is to hunker down for the long term. Absent a strong push from outside the program, things will stay that way indefinitely.

Have you ever seen a nonprofit agency that seems in a perpetual state of crisis? Chances are that what you're seeing is an agency that hasn't learned how to change itself any other way. Its organizational neurology is immature, and instead of planful change (if that isn't a word, it should be), you get a constant cycle of misfire/

resolution/misfire. Over time it does manage to reshape the old to keep up with the new, but it's hard on all concerned.

Occasionally an idea comes along that attempts to deal with this tension. Zero-based budgeting (ZBB for short) was just such an idea. The essence of ZBB is that it tried to boldly resolve the old versus new conflict by building all budgets as though they were new each year—i.e., a zero base. This is honestly a splendid idea that should work better than it does. Part of the problem is that it flies in the face of human nature as well as the physical limits of human endeavor.

There simply is inadequate time in most places to do ZBB properly, not to mention the fact that middle managers quickly tire of the yearly possibility of having what they had worked for stripped away via the stroke of some analyst's pen. Still, the idea is fundamentally sound. It gets into trouble when it becomes institutionalized and therefore beatable. Better to keep ZBB as an idea tucked away in the entrepreneurial nonprofit executive's head for judicious application.

Service Demand Versus Revenue

Demand for service versus revenue available is the granddaddy of all the tensions in nonprofit budgeting. Handled properly, it can virtually guarantee an agency solvency; muffed, it can destroy it.

The good news is that, save for legally binding or contractual situations, *most of the demand for a nonprofit's service is defined internally*. In the long run, a hospital or health care facility agrees to admit or care for only those considered appropriate by its medical and health care personnel. Museums either exhibit their own art or show others' pieces based on curatorial and managerial decisions. Theaters choose plays in similar fashion. Social service agencies choose their population according to preferences of their founders or current leaders.

Unhappily, this notion is counterintuitive. It has become a truism to talk about the growing demands on nonprofit agencies, and when the focus is on the big picture that is certainly true. The increasing problems of AIDS, homelessness, health care for an aging population, and concern for the environment combine to ratchet up the overall demand for services most often provided by nonprofit organizations. The expectation is that nonprofit organizations are overwhelmed by needs.

All of this is true primarily on a grand, sweeping scale. When it comes to an individual agency, service decisions are made on a one-at-a-time basis. Again, in the absence of legal or contractual requirements, a nonprofit agency has the ability to shape its own demand. That ability takes many forms. Every university with a waiting list for students is managing the demand for its services in a certain way. Every theater that sells tickets for its performances is managing demand, as is every substance abuse treatment center that sends counselors out to the local schools to talk with drug-abusing adolescents. The only significant questions about a particular nonprofit's demand management style are how extensive and how explicit it will be.

The good news is that the definers of demand in a nonprofit organization are its professionals. The bad news? That the gatekeepers of demand in a nonprofit organization are its professionals. The reason why this is bad news is that, for an individual program, putting nonadministrative professionals in charge of defining demand practically invites programmatic losses. Winston Churchill said that the first duty of a statesman is to get reelected. In the same way, the first duty of an executive is to insure that the organization will be around tomorrow.

Living in the Professional World

Professionals who are program directors typically live in a two-dimensional world; program (represented by the client/patient/patron) and profession (represented by himself or herself). Program unequivocally has primacy, which means that professional's job is to do everything possible in its service. If that means incurring program losses, well, these things happen.

On the other hand, professionals who are executive directors must live in a three-dimensional world, constantly balancing the demands of program, profession, and agency. No one element supercedes, which makes things confusing and messy, to say the least. What makes it hard to get it right permanently is that if any one element predominates for long periods of time the others will atrophy. Often, budget problems in a nonprofit organization are actually disguised disagreements between program directors and agency management over program goals.

I once worked with a health center that initially was considering merging with a hospital due to its failing fiscal and organizational health. Closer inspection revealed that part of its difficulty stemmed from a program director who was overspending his budget by 70 percent—while the hospital, where the program director also held a joint appointment, was using the program as a feeder to its inpatient unit. Exacerbated by lack of attention from agency management, the situation was seriously hurting the agency when all that was necessary was a more realistic realignment of both organizations' resources.

On the up side, professional standards can bring a nonprofit organization some internal strength, especially when revenue sources are demanding more for less. The fundamental service equation is inescapable: if inputs (revenues) stay the same or decline, yet outputs are expected to stay the same or go up, then the only option is to lower quality.

Nonprofit corporations, especially those in the social services, have been doing exactly that in recent years in order to cope with shrinking governmental funding. In so doing, they have illustrated the Achilles' heel of the nonprofit system. With no externally accepted "bottom line" beyond which they cannot be pushed, nonprofit service systems can and will accept funding reductions indefinitely until some externally imposed event stops the process. Until that time, they make do simply by hiring fewer or less qualified staff, paying less, accepting greater turnover, etc.

Professionals can be useful in slowing or halting this spiral by adhering to widely accepted service standards. In a sense, professionals' refusal to lower service standards in order to keep output stable forces an agency to consider change much sooner than it otherwise would! An even higher order of professionalism comes from the professional association or accrediting bodies that can threaten revocation of licensure if standards are not maintained.

They can also serve as a defense against the I'll-cut-more-than-you'll-cut competition that tempts nonprofit administrators when revenue starts drying up.

Budgeting for a nonprofit organization is simpler if you can stay away from the numbers until the last minute. What goes down in black and white is merely the technical embodiment of fundamental decisions made much earlier by executive staff and board. The secret is to make those decisions explicitly and with widespread understanding. After that, the numbers almost take care of themselves.

PART III
THE PEOPLE

CHAPTER 15

WHY THE BEST BOARDS DON'T DO ANYTHING

Dilemma. How do I write an entire chapter on boards of directors in nonprofit organizations without utterly ruining any future chance I may have of getting any board of directors anywhere in the country to hire me for anything more responsible than sweeping floors?

In truth, I don't know if there is an answer to this question other than to say what needs to be said in a straightforward fashion, as empathetically as possible, and with as few jokes as possible.

Let's start at the beginning. Boards of directors, it is generally accepted, sit atop the organization's line of authority. (Except for one executive director I know. I was interviewing with him for a job, and he asked if I wanted to see his organizational philosophy. Naturally, I said I did. He seized a copy of the organizational chart, turned it upside down, scribbled "CLIENTS" at what was now the top, and gave it to me with a flourish. I never got the job, which was probably just as well. How would I have explained to my father that I was working my way to the bottom?)

What does sitting atop the organization's line of authority mean? Administrative work involves shaping three elements of the organization: ideas, people, and technology. Generally, these three things can be thought of as the top, middle, and bottom of a pyramid, respectively. Most administrators, including boards of directors, spend most of their time dealing with one, or at most two, of these elements. That's perfectly proper, because the skills,

157

experience, and resources needed to deal with each one are very different and it makes sense for most organizations for their people to specialize. The real challenge for those in charge is making sure that the right individual or group spends most of its time trying to influence the correct element.

The Board and the Playground of Ideas

The proper role for a board of directors is to play with ideas, preferably those having to do with the agency's external environment and with internal strategies necessary for coping with the changes in that environment. With one exception—which I will get into a little later—the board's role is not to supervise staff or get involved in the details of making policy happen—the agency's technology, if you will.

Put it this way. The board of directors' job is to decide whether, what, and why. Their executives' job is to decide who, how, when, and where.

Another way of looking at the job of the board is from the perspective of time frames needed to complete tasks. Of all the parts of a nonprofit agency, the board should have the farthest time horizon. If it has to be decided by tomorrow, it isn't a matter for the board to decide. As an executive, you can put this idea into operation simply by asking yourself whether there will be a perceptible difference in the ultimate outcome of a given issue if its resolution is put off until the next meeting. If the answer is no, then the issue has the right time frame for the board's consideration. If the answer is yes, it's either not the right issue for a board or it was raised too late for the board to make a good decision.

If a nonprofit board is going to fail in its leadership role, this is one of the three most common areas in which it will happen. Often the failure is subtle and characterized more by omission than by active error. Take the issue of agency names, for example, since this is one of the few areas where at least the original board is often unequivocally more active than any staff will be.

Project Acid Head Rap Doesn't Live Here Anymore (Fortunately)

In the 1970s it was fashionable among social service agencies to name their often fledgling organizations in some memorably current way, not unlike rock music groups. This was fine for a time, and no one gave much thought to any alternative. But when the tide receded in the 1980s and 1990s many now-established agencies were left flopping on the beach with anachronistic words in their names like rap, acid, and head. What had seemed like clever marketing at the time turned out to be particularly short-term thinking.

A good mark of a board's future-directed orientation is the state of the five-year plan. It has become fashionable of late for boards and senior management to put a great deal of energy into devising five-year plans, a welcome development. But the novelty of the plan in some agencies and the sheer amount of work involved in putting one together tends to make it seem like a one-time event. Since any five-year plan is out of date fifteen minutes after it's printed and bound, the really valuable part of the whole exercise lies in incorporating a five-year time horizon (ten would be nice) into all aspects of senior management and board direction. In the words of Dwight Eisenhower (yes, Dwight Eisenhower), "Plans are nothing: planning is everything."

I said earlier that when boards fail the leadership test it usually happens in one of three areas. The second area is a bit different from failure of the vision thing, and it has to do with the director's role as a trustee of the organization. You'll know it's happening when the board starts deciding the color of the carpeting. Or the specifications of the new computer system. Or which law firm to use for the next bond issue.

I can feel heads nodding in agreement. What senior nonprofit manager hasn't felt the heavy breath of the board on his or her neck in the middle of some operational decision? To ask the question is to answer it, but that doesn't mean that kind of intervention has to be accepted passively.

Blurred as some may want it to be, for whatever reason, the distinction between the board's role and senior management's role is reasonably clear and should stay that way. Fusing the two in practice is a surefire recipe for mediocrity, if not for disaster. Why? Here is one instance where it might be helpful for all of us to spend a semester or two in law school, because lawyers have a term for this kind of behavior. It's called conflict of interest. For one party to serve as a trustee while simultaneously managing the thing that he or she has been entrusted with is an invitation to favor one role over the other. This is why, for example, banks acting as trustees for any significant capital asset establish internal controls to insure that the person acting as trustee does not also operate as a manager.

The Sock Drawer Principle

If conflict of interest seems like too strong a term, think of this as the Sock Drawer Principle. I once ran a small nonprofit corporation that did a fair amount of business with an agency of state government. One month, our single largest payment failed to arrive on time. Not having learned as yet the value of cash flow management, I did what any twenty-five-year-old manager would do in the same situation. I panicked.

The board president was out of town, so I couldn't call her. Instead, blazing with moral indignation, I went after the incompetent state agency. After some truly extensive browbeating, I managed to extract a replacement check. It wasn't until three weeks later that the board president's husband, seeing the next month's check arrive in the mail at their house, as was the custom, was reminded of something. He raced upstairs and came back down with the missing check. "This came while you were away," he said to his wife. "I knew it was important and I wanted it to be safe, so I put it in my sock drawer. I guess I forgot about it. I hope you didn't need it."

The Fort Knox Syndrome

The third major error boards tend to make is to take the fiduciary part of their responsibilities too seriously. This leads to the Fort

Knox Syndrome, where every decision is measured consciously or unconsciously according to its effect on the presumed treasures behind the barbed wire and uniformed guards. Most of the time overzealous fiduciaries exert a negative force in the name of avoiding some externally driven catastrophe. The result of their kind of thinking is most easily quantifiable if there are excess cash holdings available for investment. You can be guaranteed that the board consumed with its fiduciary obligations will sock a good portion of its holdings into Treasury bills. Treasury bills are U.S. government obligations whose main asset is the fact that if a 7.5 Richter scale earthquake leveled Washington, D.C., and left only a single typewriter operating, T-bill holders would still get paid. ("Hello, Treasury? Mind if we borrow your typewriter this evening?" "Sorry, Mr. President, gotta work on those T-bills.")

Now there's nothing inherently wrong with extremely conservative investment policies, except that the attitudes and values that shape them tend to carry over to agency mission as well, and that's when the organization begins losing out on opportunities to further its goals. It's one thing to be a concerned fiduciary, quite another to end up blocking progress in the name of responsibility. What makes this kind of obstructionism particularly difficult is that it is usually carried out with maximum sincerity. On the verge of the big vote, the board member who has sat wordlessly at the far corner of the table doing a first-rate imitation of a person with sleeping sickness for the past two years suddenly stirs and asks if it isn't illegal for a nonprofit organization to _____ (fill in the blank). Thrilled that he has finally said something, and unsure themselves whether the question is a good one, the rest of the board backpedals and spends the next six months rehashing the question all over again.

Of course, it is extremely tempting for a volunteer board to define its role in terms of tangible property only, and there is no denying that conserving assets set aside for charitable purposes is a part of the board's role. But let's be practical. If conserving property were the only reason for a board's existence, the same result could be accomplished with a net savings by turning the entire responsibility over to the trust department of a local bank.

Fortunately, there is an entrepreneurial strategy for dealing with all three of these common board lapses, and that is to *redefine the board's major responsibility as maintaining fidelity to mission,* not simply being a fiduciary to property. Focusing the board in this fashion has several advantages. For one thing, it makes it much easier to frame issues with the proper time horizon. Well-conceived missions rarely go away, and when they have to change, the signals to do so usually come from the environment with plenty of lead time to accommodate even the slowest of actors. In a related way, vehicles for accomplishing mission (i.e., programs) come and go, so the distinction between what the agency exists to do and how it has chosen to do it at a particular time can readily be made.

Most important, elevating the role of conserving fidelity to mission acts to shift the board's focus outward. Most of the board leadership failures described above entail a large amount of inward looking when what the entrepreneurial nonprofit executive needs from the board is an outward focus. Ironically, the original papers of most nonprofits suggest that an outward focus led to the organization's founding in the first place: a concern for runaway teenagers, a passion for bringing the arts to average citizens, a commitment to eliminate or minimize the impact of a specific disease.

Don't Just Do Something, Sit There

The best boards don't *do,* they think. There really is no limit to a board's effectiveness if it knows its field. Conversely, there is no more regressive force in nonprofit management than a board of directors whose collective thinking is twenty-five years behind the times. I spoke with one executive director who had spent the better part of four years working intensively with his board and was now quite justifiably pleased that they were only, in his estimate, about eight or nine years out of date.

Don't interpret this as a vicious attack on boards of directors. Why *should* they be knowledgeable about the field? One way or another, most directors come from outside of the area of nonprofit management or at least from outside of their agency's specific field; what right do we have to expect them to come with a base of knowledge? Yet that is exactly what they need if they are to be of service to their organization.

The solution is to insure that the board of directors eats, sleeps, and drinks the agency environment. How can that be accomplished when the directors' professional attentions are turned largely elsewhere? The distinguished psychiatrist Karl Menninger was fond of pointing out that if you subtract all the hours the average person spends working, taking care of personal needs, and spending time with family, there are still about forty hours left over. Your job as an entrepreneurial nonprofit executive is to claim a routine share of those forty hours.

As much as anything else, this involves systematically removing obstacles to their self-education. You could buy each one a subscription to a nonprofit-oriented publication. You could pay for them to attend special seminars in the field. You could buy them this book (hey, it's just an idea). You could do literally dozens of things to encourage board members to learn about their professionally adopted field, but they all share the same theme that your role is to make it easier. No board member should have to incur a dime of extra expense if he or she doesn't want to, and the time involved should be as tailored to his or her individual needs as possible. After all, the members have already demonstrated some sort of motivation to serve, even if it's just that their boss wants them to, and it shouldn't be too hard to learn about and then capitalize on that motivation.

Some Investment Advice

Speaking of motivation, you will want to ask yourself, "What makes a good board member?" For some guidance you might want to look at how the for-profit sector puts a board together. And when you do, you will find some interesting patterns. On any given for-profit board you might find venture capitalists, part-owners, brothers or sisters of the chief executive, vice presidents of the organization, or representatives of major players in related industries. This is a board membership model that non-profits could well stand to imitate.

Why? Because all of these types of board members have one thing in common: *investment.* They all have quite sensible and usually intimately personal reasons for serving on the board. Often the investment is a literal one, but sometimes it is a figurative or nonfinancial investment too. Either way, they have reasons to be passionately concerned with the direction of the company.

For obvious reasons nonprofit organizations cannot imitate most of these kinds of investments on board members' parts. Still, it's an instructive comparison. The key is that for most for-profit board members the corporation's success will enhance them in some way while its failure will diminish them. It is harder to achieve that kind of connection in a nonprofit organization, but not impossible. Again, the answer is to assemble the board according to its sense of investment in the mission of the organization, not so much the organization itself.

The usual way of creating a nonprofit board is to pick a lawyer, a member of the clergy, a banker, a consumer representative, etc. Forget it. Quotas are for salespeople. Picking board members solely according to what type of graduate school they happened to attend gets you nowhere. Instead, do it the entrepreneurial way. Envision where you want the organization to be in five years (ten if you can manage it). Then look for some people who are there *right now*.

I did this kind of thing in a modest way when I was running my first nonprofit organization. Because my board at the time was homogeneously suburbanite, it looked to the rest of the world as if I were pursuing my clergy quota when I tried to recruit a local minister. And in fact I greatly valued his patience and intelligence, and I agreed with the veterans that it never hurts to have a person of the cloth on your side. But the thing that really distinguished him was that he was patient, intelligent, highly respected, and controlled just the right amount of low-rent office space for my corporation. (It worked. He couldn't join the board, but later on we rented his space).

A less concrete and self-serving example. Many years ago an

association I worked for collectively realized that at some point in the future we were going to have to produce cold, hard economic benefits for our nonprofit corporation members in addition to our more glamorous efforts at advocacy and organization. One of the first things we did was to add a gentleman to our board who, unlike virtually everyone else, had had experience as a bona fide successful private sector entrepreneur. When crunch time finally came several years later, he was comfortably installed as president and fully capable of making the hard economic choices.

The problem with quotas, stated or implied, is that they tend to be based on credentials or outward labels, which in turn are rooted in the member's technical skills. Inevitably, then, the quota approach gets everyone to thinking how he or she can *do* something for the organization, and that violates the sock drawer principle. Quotas encourage lawyers to think like lawyers, accountants like accountants, and so on. Ultimately this is regressive. To offset it, entrepreneurial executives seek broad thinkers who happen to be trained as lawyers, engineers, etc. Moreover, they seek out board members who may have something to contribute to the group's future, not who will just be distinguished citizens from its past.

Many of these prescriptions may sound like recommendations for boards composed solely of other nonprofit administrators, and in fact many agencies I know have found these types to be extremely valuable members. However, as a class of board member, nonprofit and government sorts should probably be more yeast than flour. For that matter, so should most other classes of prospective board members. Because from the standpoint of the organization, a carefully homogenized board is like eating scrambled eggs three times a day—it gets boring pretty fast and in the long run it's definitely not healthy.

What Size?

Why do we insist on building boards the way the pharaohs built the pyramids—putting together great masses of humanity, equipping them poorly, training them less, and laying in a heavy supply of whips? Few traditions are more firmly established than the one that says nonprofits must have large boards of directors. Yet if you read any serious student of group work you'll find limited group size a consistent theme. Small groups act faster, negotiate better, and are easier to shape into a coherent entity than larger groups.

There are two major reasons why nonprofit organizations have large boards, other than vague tradition. One is that there is presumably a prestige component to membership on a board, and it seems an easy and relatively harmless reward to bestow on some deserving citizen. The board member whose name is on the list purely for its marquee value also falls into this category. Politicians and civic leaders are the usual coconspirators here, and it's normally a benign device, fooling no one except perhaps the named luminary who now at least feels guilty if he or she doesn't return the director's phone calls. Which of course may be why he or she was put on the letterhead in the first place.

The second bad reason for oversized nonprofit boards is one to which I will plead guilty of having used on occasion. Let me illustrate it by saying that if my life depended on my being able to plunge a given group into total disarray within an hour, I would much rather try it with a group of thirty than with a group of three. Large boards—indeed, large functional groups of any kind—spend their lives on the brink of haplessness, and it doesn't take much for a determined executive to push them over that brink. And when that happens, whose power and influence are certain to fill the vacuum? You guessed it.

So what is the right size? Seven would be nice. Nine would be okay too, but however many you choose, be sure to add two to the number you really want to have present in order to make up for the members who sickness and weather are sure to keep away from every meeting. And make sure that the total is an odd number. After the thunderous arguments about the agency's mission, the last thing you want is a tie vote.

Fund-raising in a nonprofit organization is like the mice that wanted to tie a bell around the cat's neck. Everyone agrees that it's a terrific idea, but no one wants to be the one who actually does it. I have lost count of the number of nonprofit staff members who tell me that it is an explicit condition of board membership that directors do—or do not—fund raise. If there is any single thing that is more likely to set many board members' teeth on edge it is the slightest hint that they will be expected to raise money for the organization. Yet there is no denying the reality that most nonprofits need the capital base and the operational flexibility that fund raising can provide.

May I suggest a simple way to end this conflict wherever it occurs? *Fund raising should be done by those who are good at fund raising.* If the people who are good at fund raising happen to be on the staff, fine. If they happen to be on the board, that's fine too (fund raising being one of the few areas where the Sock Drawer Principle doesn't apply).

This simple idea is really just a matter of applying basic principles of personnel management to board issues. We wouldn't expect a plumber to be able to install carpeting, so why expect someone completely devoid of fund-raising experience to suddenly become a fund raiser by virtue of his or her membership on the board of directors?

Two caveats here. The first is that no board member should expect to get off the hook just by submitting a notarized physician's statement attesting to a congenital inability to raise funds. There needs to be clear and compelling evidence, and the only real way of getting it is to try out the board member with a few fund-raising gigs. Second, the board as a whole needs some involvement in the fund-raising effort, so neither should the whole group be excused just because of a handful of individuals. The entrepreneurial way to solve this problem is to broaden the definition of fund raising. In actuality, fund raising is composed of many parts, and you can take advantage of this fact to design a personalized development program for each board member. When the challenge is defined as developing the organization, individual directors uncomfortable with traditional face-to-face fund raising can find a perfectly productive role by, say, allowing a creative use of their underused beach house, or by introducing their affluent friends to the nonprofit's Designated Fund Raiser, or by simply standing and pointing in the general direction of some good prospects.

What Board Members Should Not Lie Awake Nights Worrying About

Nearly every prospective board member with a subscription to at least one popular magazine or newspaper is going to have the same question: *Am I going to get sued?* Even if it's not spoken in exactly that fashion, the question will always be there. Naturally, the answer can never be an unequivocal no. No matter how well run the agency may be, one always has to accept the possibility that someone at some point will file suit against it for some reason, and that that suit will eventually touch each member of the board.

This having been said, however, the nonprofit executive knows that much of the fear of civil lawsuits on the part of the board of directors is wasted energy. To understand why this is the case, let's do a little historical digging and then a bit of hard analysis.

To begin with, lawsuits filed against boards of directors of any kind are a relatively recent development in American society. They really got their start in the for-profit sector earlier this century and then got rolling in the '70s and '80s with the advent of massive takeovers, mergers, acquisitions, and buyouts, as well as the evolution of product liability laws. Often, suits against directors came from a corporation's own "members"—i.e., its shareholders—based on the accusation that the board had somehow breached its fiduciary duty of maximizing stockholders' wealth. For example, boards were often sued as a result of accepting a lower buyout price than some felt was possible. And of course product liability lawsuits targeted boards with the argument that they should have prevented the alleged anticonsumer decisions from being made in the first place.

Neither condition has a nonprofit analog. Tax-exempt organizations by definition have no stockholders, and the majority produce no tangible product (we'll come to liability for services later). Understand also that there are sometimes two additional motivators for board suits, those being that the suit is part of a larger strategic plan for corporate advantage and that Fortune 500-type companies usually have board members who are just plain juicy targets for any lawsuit seeking monetary damages anyway.

Clearly there is little parallel in the nonprofit world. While many nonprofit organizations' boards may include individuals of some means, few are likely to represent the same kind of intensive collection of wealth as would a large public corporation's board.

Another factor in favor of the average board member is that it's extremely difficult to draw a straight legal line between some sort of civil wrong and the action or inaction of a volunteer board of directors. The line is easier to draw in the medical world, and in fact board liability in the medical world is often a separate story from other nonprofits entirely, but it still takes the average plaintiff a lot of time and money to pursue it.

There is yet another disincentive working against lawsuits against boards. English common law had a well-accepted principle that quasi-public money such as one finds in tax-exempt organizations should not be siphoned off to private pockets, even in the form of compensation for civil wrongs. In some states this general principle has actually become codified in the form of a law granting partial or total protection from lawsuits. In Massachusetts, for example, this Charitable Immunity Statute severely limits the public charity's exposure to monetary damages. Recently non-profit advocates strengthened the statute by providing volunteer board members total protection against liability except in three very narrowly defined areas. Check to see if you have a similar provision in your state.

The most profound source of protection of all is the nature of legal liability. A critical element in findings of professional liability, which is the type of lawsuit that most board members fear, is that the defendant(s) deviated from some generally accepted standard of care. So tell board members to cheer up. To put it bluntly, if there is no generally accepted standard of care in the nonprofit's field (as is the case with most nonmedical nonprofits), it's going to be real hard for someone to prove that the board deviated from it.

In spite of all this rational left-brain stuff, it is still going to be hard to convince most board members that their risk of being on the wrong end of a civil lawsuit is low. And, as mentioned, there are no guarantees anyhow. It almost seems as if nonprofit board members bring a certain quota of worry with them to the job. So try to peel some of those layers of worry aside and find out exactly why they are frightened. With the right amount of casual discussion you can probably get to the heart of it, and it will sound something like this: *I'm worried that doing this good deed will somehow get me in trouble and I'll end up losing my house, my property, and my good name.*

Unlikely? Yes. Impossible? Absolutely not. In fact, there are some classic ways that nonprofit board members can find themselves in this kind of horror story—and one major thing you can do to prevent it.

What Board Members *Should* Lie Awake Nights Worrying About

One thing that no law or unwritten rule can protect volunteer board members from is prosecution for criminal acts. Embezzlement is embezzlement even if it occurs in an art museum or a university hospital. Directors intent on criminal action can and should be apprehended. Of course, directors intent on criminal action aren't likely to be the type to lie awake nights worrying about their board role. But the point should be made that criminal behavior has no protection deriving from the tax-exempt form of business organization.

If you have board members prone to worrying, focus them on the area where it could count for something: tax and benefit withholdings. One of the ingenious things about the American system of business is that employers do a lot of bookkeeping for others. They calculate money destined for government bank accounts and then withhold it from employees' paychecks for a few days. They take money from employees' paychecks and pay for health insurance with it. And they promise to make various payments on employees' behalf to things like pension programs and other employee benefits.

On occasion, cash gets tight in a nonprofit agency and certain payments need to slip behind schedule. Since most of the average agency's assets go home every night, the wise manager seeks to avoid unfriendly gestures like missing a payroll. One very tempting way to hold back some cash is to put off making a tax payment. Or a health insurance premium. Or an unemployment insurance premium. Unfortunately, by the time the money supply is replenished, there is often another irresistible demand that takes precedence over paying those now overdue taxes. And then perhaps the whole cycle gets repeated again a few weeks later, and before long the organization has a serious problem on its hands.

New York Times writer Claudia Deutsch tells of an executive on the board of a nonprofit agency who had to spend five thousand dollars in legal fees to fight off an IRS attempt to collect his share of ninety thousand dollars from unremitted employee withholding payments. Well, with all due respect, I would suggest that anyone purporting to call himself an executive who allows a nonprofit agency to try to work its way out of a jam by stiffing the IRS ought to have his car phone yanked and be forced to pay for his own subscription to the *Wall Street Journal*. To say that the agency's mission is more important than these most basic of responsibilities is merely to perpetuate poor management in the guise of dedication.

Happily, the solution to this problem also happens to solve a number of other problems as well. *Insist that board members not check their business acumen at the door.* There seems to be something about a nonprofit board meeting that turns otherwise rock solid business judgment to mush. Why should we expect the economics governing the nonprofit's environment to behave differently simply because the entity has been granted tax-exempt status? The answer, of course, is that we shouldn't, and the director who insists that his or her agency exercise sound business judgment in all facets of its operations is providing the greatest service of all.

CHAPTER 16

ARE YOU AN ENTREPRENEURIAL NONPROFIT EXECUTIVE?

The next time you attend a conference with your peers, look around the room. If my experience is any guide, you will see a handful of truly entrepreneurial nonprofit executives. They may be executive directors, assistant executive directors, people in charge of administration, or people responsible for programs. They may be lower in the executive ranks, or perhaps they haven't even entered them yet. It doesn't matter where in the organizational chart they appear because they always share many of the same characteristics and accomplish similar things on behalf of their agencies.

Progress in any field depends largely on the work of a handful of practitioners positioned, by choice or by chance, on the leading edge of change. It is the entrepreneurial drive that puts certain executives on that leading edge and gives them the force to move the whole field forward. From them we can derive the greatest improvements in program and management technology.

Can the nonentrepreneurial executive push us forward and teach us about the field? Yes, but only in bits and pieces, and then only by chance. The entrepreneurial director tests the limits in a coherent, cogent fashion and shows us how to expand them for the benefit of mission.

Understanding what the entrepreneurial nonprofit executive is and how he or she works will benefit us all, because it is entirely possible for the rest of us to apply selected entrepreneurial techniques and approaches without attempting a wholesale retooling of our executive style.

173

The word "entrepreneurial" as used here has nothing to do with money. Instead, it refers to mission-centered activity entered into for the purpose of creating opportunity for some or all aspects of the tax-exempt organization. Naturally, money does enter into the equation early on, usually as an initial outlay that may (or may not) result in subsequent direct benefit. It must also be noted that the net effect of the entrepreneurial executive's efforts must result in a positive financial benefit to the agency. Which is a stilted way of saying that the agency makes money.

Individual entrepreneurial efforts by themselves need not be profitable, and in fact it is all but certain that many will not be. Some will be tentative feelers, others will produce measurable benefit years later, and still others will be downright failures. The charm (and the effectiveness) of the entrepreneurial nonprofit executive flows from the skilled mixing of outcomes.

Corporate structure has little to do with entrepreneurial activity. Some of the entrepreneurial nonprofit executives I have encountered chose a nonprofit vehicle for all of their activity, while others created for-profit subsidiaries. Whenever the circumstances demanded creation of a new enterprise, however, the effective executives were careful to insure themselves exactly as much control over the new organization as was necessary.

Entrepreneurial is not the same as "good" or "hard-working." This field has more than its share of bright, organized, hard-working individuals who are good coordinators and can motivate staff to perform well; I know, I have met scores. But, as desirable as these characteristics are, they are simply a different collection of talents from those the entrepreneurial nonprofit executive brings to his or her job.

Warning: the entrepreneurial nonprofit executive type is not an unmixed blessing. There is a dark side to the accomplishments of which it is capable. Carried to an extreme, the entrepreneurial executive instinct can leave an agency vulnerable or even destroy it altogether. Of course, so can an excess of caution, the chief difference being that the former destroys it unequivocally while the latter merely robs its soul.

What characterizes the entrepreneurial nonprofit executive as a type? I have seen a number of key traits or situational characteristics in these leaders; most of the nonprofit executives I would consider entrepreneurial have possessed a good share of the ones that follow. Ask yourself these questions:

Are you full-time? Part-time executive leadership usually means big-time trouble. The exception is the young nonprofit agency struggling to get on its feet, but even here the arrangement needs to become full-time as soon as practical. There was a period several years ago when lots of nonprofits seemed to have part-timers at the helm, but in recent years the trend is more toward full-time leadership.

Still, I would rather have the explicit part-time director than the formerly entrepreneurial director who can't let go and is now shared by two or more corporations. I have run into this insidious arrangement a surprising number of times, often in the health field. One health center I worked with employed a physician who had founded the place and who appeared to the outside world to be the organization's director. In reality, he was split between the nearby hospital staff and the health center, where he saw patients and did a small amount of administration. The result was that the center spent several years with no executive focus and eventually found that its environment had changed so dramatically that it needed to merge with a larger group in order to preserve its service system.

Another visionary had founded a treatment center for abused boys which he ran full-time for about ten years before getting interested in building a nursing home for severely disabled youths. Eventually he started spending the bulk of his time at the nursing home, turning over responsibility for the center to his former assistant director while retaining his executive director title and a certain executive aura with no day-to-day responsibilities.

What happened was predictable. The arrangement worked well during a period of generalized growth in the field of abuse services. Then both the demand and the ability to pay for these services leveled off and the effects of the executive vacuum at the treatment center began to show up, masquerading as budget problems. Budget cut after budget cut failed to solve the problem, understandably enough since the real issue was not spending but the lack of executive vision. Eventually, the center was also forced to consider massive reorganization, including the possibility of merging with another agency just to keep the services going.

Are you a coexecutive director? If so, start restructuring. Tomorrow morning. The only place where two steering wheels work well is on big fire trucks.

Does the next decade seem like the blink of an eye to you? Easily the most striking characteristic of the entrepreneurial directors I have encountered is their future orientation. Where others see months and years, these executives see decades. What looks to others like sharp upturns and downturns in fortune are for them more like rolling plains.

They are more likely to feel frantic when their projected pace of change is greater than the time they have available to accommodate it than when, say, a major grant proposal is coming due. One particularly entrepreneurial executive director I met laid out his vision for his agency in five-year blocks for me, then confided that his biggest worry was that he saw more blocks of years than he had blocks of working time remaining.

For an idea of how the executives' orientation differs from others', ask them all what day they spend most of their time thinking about. Their answers should look like the following table:

WHAT "DAY" IS IT?

Position	Answer
Accountant	Yesterday
Program worker	Today
Manager	Tomorrow
Executive director	Five years from today

One very big payoff of this orientation is that the executive stays focused, never getting distracted or discouraged by small successes or failures which he or she rightfully considers momentary blips in a longer-term path. Events happen in a kind of slow motion which makes strategic responses easier. The entrepreneurial nonprofit executive understands that he or she can only control the future, not the past, and that it is when upcoming realities are in their formative stage that they can be shaped most easily.

Obviously, this ability to see things in the longer term is intimately connected with the executive's visionary style. Events and their consequences seem to spread out like a panorama, and the interrelationships among them give texture to the whole picture. It's hard to imagine learning this skill—it seems innate— but a longer time orientation would be a good place to start moving along the entrepreneurial learning curve.

Do you tend to think in terms of concepts and strategies? It is simply a fact of life that the most powerful people in any field spend most of their time dealing with ideas, leaving technical and supervisory duties to others. For a field so people-oriented as nonprofit management, this would seem to be inadvisable, but actually it makes a great deal of sense. To start with, few of those working for a nonprofit organization outside of the executive ranks are likely to have the time or inclination to think about their jobs conceptually. A harried, economically pressed environment encourages short-term thinking, which in turn leads to temporary results. Temporary results wear off fast, necessitating more short-term thinking and more frenzied activity. This produces respect ("Oh, he works so *hard*") but few results.

Ironically, most entrepreneurial nonprofit executives' "people skills" are more than adequate, occasionally even brilliant. But an executive style built around people without an appreciation for the way they fit into larger, interrelated systems is guaranteed to be ineffectual.

The same is true for technical matters. Thinking and acting solely in the area of personal or technical matters means defining the future as the next person on the appointment calendar or the next technical problem. By thinking his or her way out of this self-limiting approach, the entrepreneurial nonprofit executive can begin marking out a future for the organization that offers the possibility for strong entrepreneurial action.

Have you been (or are you planning to stay) on the job for a long time? For many reasons, entrepreneurial executives usually answer this question with a yes. This may partly be due to the amount of time it takes to create real and permanent change in the nonprofit environment, but certainly it is related to executives' tendency to think in extended time frames. Why stay in a nice place for a long weekend when you can make it a month?

Several of the executives I have met claimed they had originally planned to stay a much shorter time. It's difficult to evaluate such retrospective comments, but I tend to take them at face value. While most entrepreneurial types have an almost palpable restlessness, it is probably the directing of that energy into the corporation itself that keeps them in place for so long.

Did you start the organization, or does your arrival now appear to outsiders to be a distinct break with the past? Here the English language fails us. It is not merely that the entrepreneurial nonprofit executive is identified with the organization, but that they are "of" each other.

To understand what this means, consider the business world. The two things that change proprietary entities most dramatically are technology and people. With technology so utterly irrelevant to the delivery of most nonmedical nonprofits' services, the unequivocal driving force is the people leading them, and the entrepreneurial nonprofit executive is always the single most powerful person among them.

Perhaps this explains why so many hugely talented people voluntarily forgo greater material rewards for the pleasure of managing a nonprofit. Let's not get sappy about it, though. We're talking about power here. The opportunity to be a chief executive officer, entrepreneurial or not, may account for some of the professional charm of our sector. In a small business of equivalent size, reaching the top position generally requires investing personal money, either to purchase the business or to start it. In addition, start-ups and the very smallest of businesses will require the chief to possess some level of technical skill so as to get the work done while marketing it at the same time. Where else but in tax-exempt organizations can an ordinary person secure a top management job on the strength of managerial ability alone and without putting down some cash?

One characteristic that nonprofit entrepreneurs share with their for-profit colleagues is that they usually don't repeat their performance. For one thing, they probably don't have the time. More profoundly, there is a depth of connectedness between the executive and his or her agency that is extremely difficult to repeat. The result is that resigning to create another agency is about as easy as recreating oneself.

Did you cause your agency to grow? The entrepreneurial nonprofit executive understands that growth in every sense of the word is essential for survival. Many entrepreneurial executives lead their organizations through at least one period of explosive growth by orchestrating the convergence of service need, funding source, and internal capacity. The rest choose slow, steady growth over time.

The real success in causing a nonprofit agency to grow comes from leading it through a period of evolution that I call the Bermuda Triangle of Growth. This is the range of budget size in which strange and mysterious things seem to happen to nonprofits, the range where they are too big to be small anymore, but too small to be big. Like its real-life counterpart, this Triangle is filled with peril. Enter it with the thought of staying there, and you will quietly disappear.

Many cope with the Triangle by avoiding it, always staying just under the minimum size for entry. (A million dollars in volume? Two million? It varies by service type, geography, and dozens of other variables. Give me a team of graduate students and a good computer system and I'll figure out what it is for you.)

Instinctively, the entrepreneurial nonprofit executive understands that his or her agency has to grow through this dangerous period quickly, like a stone skipping across water. Beyond avoiding the organizational equivalent of gawky teenager-like growth, the concrete reward for getting through the Triangle is irresistible for the entrepreneurial nonprofit executive: a bona fide, full-time second in command. Call this person a deputy, an assistant executive director, or whatever, the reward for emerging from the period is the enormously useful capacity to delegate line authority to someone else who can reasonably be expected to see the Big Picture also, not just the programmatic or financial one.

It may be exactly this step which enables the entrepreneurial executive to work his or her magic. Until this point, the director was expected to be all things to all people and to do all things equally well, a convenient fiction that no one believed but that suited various players' purposes to uphold. Getting a real second not only gives the director additional time, it is the first substantive step toward relinquishing day-to-day control. As such, it is both a real and symbolic development because the executive who is most comfortable spreading his or her arms and touching both sides of the agency will never be an entrepreneur.

Does growth mean only revenue growth? Absolutely not, although there's a subtle distinction worth making here. Increasing revenue for its own sake is never a goal or even a good measure of an entrepreneurial executive. Conversely, the mere presence of positive, sustained growth by itself does not signal an entrepreneurial executive since under many conditions competence alone is enough to accomplish growth.

Yet real growth in agency revenue is a valid partial indicator of entrepreneurial thinking because entrepreneurial accomplishments almost certainly cause overall revenue to increase as a side effect. Again, the point is that dedication to mission comes first, and financial success follows from it.

Are you comfortable dealing with the world outside your agency in all its forms—but do you truly prefer being in the agency? Entrepreneurial nonprofit executives deal with U.S. senators as easily as with cab drivers, with local business people as with Hollywood figures. Some are more than a little successful at being the glad-hander. But they seem to do so mainly because they have to, not because they enjoy it. One gets the distinct impression that, on the whole, the entrepreneurial nonprofit executive would always rather be back at the agency *because that's where the important things get done.*

Do you assume that the world is against your agency? (Or at least that no one cares whether you succeed or not?) The most subjective of all the entrepreneur's characteristics, this one comes from some unimaginably deep wellspring of survival instinct. It's the thing that makes for 3 A.M. awakenings and that promotes a sixth sense about dangers in the agency environment. It's almost a starting point, a strategic assumption that causes the executive and everyone else to take nothing for granted.

There is an implied logic that old-fashioned nonprofit management takes to heart. It goes something like this: Everyone wants good works; we are doing good works; therefore, everyone wants us. Fewer rude shocks are available to the neophyte nonprofit executive than the discovery that this conclusion does not necessarily follow from the above premises.

Not paranoia but rather a kind of healthy pragmatism, the expectation that the world will produce an endless series of obstacles for the nonprofit to overcome in order to do its good works can also help minimize employee burnout by setting realistic expectations. Not coincidentally, it helps focus everyone and it fosters a shared sense of unity and purpose. The entrepreneurial nonprofit executive knows that if guns must be drawn, it's better that they all be pointed outside the organization.

Do you have a small board? Entrepreneurial nonprofit executives seem to discover early on that they need a small board of directors. Small boards allow the executive to concentrate on developing the mission without spending undue energy on trivial discussions or resolving disputes. Small boards tend to reduce posturing as well, so those who might serve on the board mainly so that others can see them serving on the board will be inclined to go elsewhere.

Managed properly, a small board of directors overseeing an entrepreneurial executive can add immeasurably to the quality of services just by forcing the executive and his or her staff to *think*. One board of a youth-service agency I know used to have board meetings that ran late into the night as members and the executive argued furiously with each other over the likely direction of juvenile justice in the coming decade.

Another advantage to small boards is that it's harder for average directors to hide (don't show this piece to a prospective board member). Their presence is far more likely to be felt and their absence noted when the board numbers a handful than when a board meeting looks like the seats behind home plate in the World Series.

Those inclined to worry about such things will fret that small boards will only rubber-stamp an entrepreneurial director, thereby losing one of the few checks and balances on a potentially dangerous chief executive. While this may seem plausible, it is a misplaced fear. The real rubber stamp in the hands of an unscrupulous executive director is an oversized, apparently "representative" board since it provides a good cover while its sheer bulk gives the shrewd manipulator plenty of room to isolate critics. Small board failures to carry out fiduciary oversight, on the other hand, are usually due to the personalities involved and not the board's structure.

Do you know what you don't know? Finally, almost all of the entrepreneurial nonprofit executives I have met succeed because they know what it is that they don't know. Every administrator has blind spots, but the entrepreneurial nonprofit executive turns what would otherwise be liabilities into assets by seeking out complementary skills in his or her staff. Often, although by no means always, what entrepreneurial nonprofit executives don't know is financial management. Frequently they are not detail-oriented enough, and occasionally program concerns are their weak areas. Whatever it is, they are sure to find someone whose knowledge and expertise dovetails with their own and then give them the latitude to get the job done.

It may be misleading to suggest that the entrepreneurial non-profit executive succeeds because he or she knows how to delegate. But it is only slightly misleading. The effectiveness of the executive comes from his or her understanding that real control derives not from involvement in daily minutiae but from the ability to see the need for change. Pairing this vision thing with the knack for sensing opportunities in change, and you have the makings of an entrepreneurial nonprofit executive.

The next time you attend that conference of your peers and look around the room, count the small number that are truly entrepreneurial nonprofit directors, and then count the number that have adopted at least a handful of entrepreneurial characteristics.

Is one of them you?

CHAPTER 17

EMPLOYEES: PAYING, KEEPING, GETTING

When the entrepreneurial nonprofit executive director looks backward at the history of the nonprofit labor force—a hard thing to
do, for looking backward is not in the executive's nature—here is
what he or she sees:

- A plentiful supply of young, often college-educated people
  ready and willing to touch the world through nonprofit
  works.
- An overall work force reasonably well educated, even at the
  lowest level.
- Pay scales that rivaled their government counterparts and at
  least allowed for a decent if modest standard of living.
- Relatively low turnover.

When looking ahead to the coming decade and beyond, here is
what he or she sees:

- A drop in the number of eighteen-year-olds entering the work
  force so dramatic that 1989 levels will not be reached again
  until the year 2003.
- Increased competition for educated workers who can exercise
  independent thought.
- A shortage of entry-level personnel.
- An abundance of people qualified for mid-career and senior
  positions.

In short, it will be a very different world for those trying to recruit and retain employees for nonprofit groups.

Pyramid Versus Circle

If the employee recruitment world is going to be more competitive and begin to change in major ways, the average nonprofit corporation enters it with certain very exploitable advantages. Organizational style is one of them.

The modern organizational model in all its rational, hierarchical, pyramid-shaped glory grew out of the work of Frederick Winslow Taylor. Practically speaking, it was stamped on the minds and hearts of virtually all people holding positions of power from the '40s through the early '70s by the experience of World War II, which was necessarily a hierarchical, mass-production affair. More important, we won. Consequently, huge masses of people's single most successful organizational experience came about in the unique circumstances of a national war effort.

During the postwar years we applied our mass production lessons to the creation of economic power unlike anything the world had ever seen. But during the '60s and '70s, we began losing our manufacturing base to foreign competitors, and from that loss came the beginnings of unease with the way we had been doing things. Since that time, and increasingly since the 1980s, there has been a public questioning of the traditional form of business organization. Today, hierarchy and its cousin, bureaucracy, are regarded by many as Exhibit One in the case against Western-style business.

Boosted by the evolving demands of the information age, a new image of organization as web is replacing that of organization as pyramid, according to Sally Helgesen, author of *The Female Advantage: Women's Ways of Leadership*. The idea is that there is no up or down in these organizations. What connects people in this model is not an abstract line of authority but direct and multiply connected circuitry very much like, ironically, a computer microchip.

If this kind of shift is really beginning to happen—and in the leading industries it is—then nonprofit organizations will have a marked advantage in recruiting tomorrow's employees because most of today's nonprofits are already more web than pyramid. Take the relationship between the average chief executive pay and the average hourly manufacturing worker pay, for example. If pay is a reasonable signal of distance from top to bottom—and what could be a better one?—then American companies are phenomenally hierarchical, with *Business Week* magazine calculating that the average CEO is paid *ninety-three times* more than the average entry-level hourly worker. The comparable multiple in the nonprofit world, according to The Technical Assistance Center's 1990 survey of nonprofit wages and benefits, is five.

Let's pause long enough to permit candor to catch up with us. To the extent that nonprofits have been web-style organizational structures in the past, it has usually been because the groups were small or tightly geographically focused, or because they couldn't afford multiple layers of administration anyway. Organizational theory had little to do with it. Fine. The point is that business entities are changing because economic and other conditions in the external environment are making it in their interest to change, not because a handful of business magazines said it was the smart thing to do. Nonprofit groups that move consciously and explicitly in this direction are positioning themselves to be attractive to and understandable by the employee of tomorrow.

Getting Them Over the Threshold

The old salesman's creed was simple: *Get 'em over the threshold.* There's a nugget of truth in that motto for nonprofit employers as well, for getting quality employees is going to be more difficult in the future than it has ever been in the past. Yet, once exposed, many people get addicted to the kind of public service a nonprofit or government entity can offer and never cross back over that threshold. If you disbelieve it, look at the numbers of foundation executives, U.S. senators, and other notables that the heady early days of the Peace Corps produced. A disproportionately high share, I am sure.

As employers, most nonprofit corporations have voracious appetites for employees, and the entrepreneurial nonprofit executive knows how to feed his or her machine. Like many other successful practices, the executive performs this one long before it's necessary. What he or she does is more art than science, but it is worth dissecting a bit for the elements that others can copy. Here are a few.

Segment Your Employee Market

Consciously or not, entrepreneurial nonprofit executives segment their employee market sources and allocate their recruitment resources accordingly. There are many different ways of segmenting the employee market, but the most useful seems to be along a continuum from commodity to specialty. That is, employees hired in large numbers ought to be sought in the same ways one would acquire commodities, while recruitment techniques for one-of-a-kind positions need to be handled in an individually tailored fashion.

Note that the commodity-specialty continuum is not necessarily equivalent to the professional-nonprofessional continuum. A nonprofit organization needing dozens of pediatricians needs to develop mass recruitment strategies, while the nonprofit, Ph.D.-rich think tank has a much different problem finding a custodian. Fortune 500-type companies demonstrate the commodity recruitment approach when they annually comb through thousands of MBA candidates to fill the ten positions they have available.

Segmenting your employee market means knowing where and how to look for employees. As much as anything else, it means knowing what your agency does well when it comes to recruiting and retaining employees, and then capitalizing on it. It means taking concrete steps such as deciding ahead of time which positions are best recruited through word of mouth and which through advertising in professional journals. It means setting policies for determining when to use metropolitan dailies versus local papers versus radio stations; when to use college placement offices or headhunters; and when to use trade schools. Above all, it means knowing when to break all of the rules you just set so carefully.

Advertise Smart

Success in paid job advertising is a game of millimeters. A page of help wanted ads is so noisy ("Pick me! Pick me!" "Lookee here!" "Forget *them,* read *me!*" "Yoohoo!" "LOOK AT ME") that standing out just a little bit is a monumental effort. You need a clutter cutter.

Fortunately, the advertising world produces its own clutter cutters, better known as advertising agencies. If you do any substantial amount of advertising, it pays to use an agency. Why? Very simply, they're better at it than you are. They do what they do forty hours a week, not six times a year.

Need more reasons? Advertising agencies are usually free. Newspapers give them a discount in return for their volume of placements. When the agency charges you full freight, the discount they get from the newspaper becomes their payment.

Using an agency is also easier. They have all the equipment and skills under a single roof, and the really good ones can listen to what you want and translate it into a finished product. Your reach across a given geographic area can be far greater with less effort via their networks and advertising protocols, and their more intimate knowledge of the advertising world stretches your dollar (this message not brought to you by The Advertising Council).

Hunt a Few Heads

Headhunters are slowly beginning to discover the nonprofit world, and vice versa, and for a certain few positions using a headhunter may be a viable option. The main reasons why headhunters have not been used much in the nonprofit world are their cost and the we–don't–do–it–that–way syndrome. On the other hand, hiring the wrong person for a top position is far more costly than any fee a headhunter may charge, so the option should not be dismissed out of hand. Some headhunters will do a nonprofit search pro bono as a mixture of community service and business development.

For lower-level staff in a hard employee market, consider temporary services. Again this can be a costly approach, but if the alternative is no or inappropriate staff, it may be worth it. If the employee becomes permanent the temporary agency charges a fee, often on a conversion schedule that spreads the cost over six to twelve weeks. In the end you pay about the same as if you had paid the full fee up front, but you get some time to assess the fit.

Get Lost in a Few Crowds

Every section of a good book needs some suspense, and the suspense for the next few paragraphs will be whether I can get through them without using that bedraggled term from the '80s, *networking*. Here goes.

If you're interested in recruiting staff, get out of the office. The only employees you'll see around there are ones you've already hired. More on how to use those folks in a moment, but the point is that the recruiting function must be externally focused.

One of the smartest things I ever saw in the employee recruitment area was accomplished by a small but growing nonprofit with headquarters just off the downtown area of a small town. Needing a billing clerk, they hired a woman who lived down the street. It turns out that she was a devout churchgoer with lots of friends in her religious circle, and the next time there was an administrative vacancy, she suggested one of her friends. This friend then suggested a mutual churchgoing friend for the next new administrative opening, and the executive director caught onto his recruitment gold mine. By the time they had exhausted the ladies' church circle, a good handful of them were in place in administrative openings throughout the agency.

The key to word-of-mouth (and therefore less costly) recruiting is tapping into ready-made circles of friends and colleagues. In other words, it's not who you know, it's who you get to know. The entrepreneurial executive makes a point of knowing how to tap into local channels for new employees, especially those in the fastest-growing segments of the population. The process of tapping in can be hastened along by offering existing employees rewards for referring their friends.

Grow Your Own

Of course, the very best entrepreneurial recruitment strategy is to grow your own employees. It's no accident that hospitals at one time trained large numbers of nurses. They *needed* large numbers of nurses to make things work. The tangible and intangible benefits of training future employees are hard to overestimate.

While hospital-style nursing programs are within reach of only a limited number of nonprofit organizations, the underlying principles are applicable by all regardless of size. For instance, I know of a nursing home administrator who in the 1970s started a small program in which he would pay the tuition for existing nurses' aides to obtain LPN training. A key decision was to attach no requirements forcing successful graduates to work at the home for a period of time after graduation, a provision which his board initially resisted.

Although the administrator's motives seem on the surface to be equally as noble as they are naive—why assist someone to get training without requiring anything in return?—they were actually brilliantly entrepreneurial. The nursing home was the largest employer in its rural area, and generally recognized as the best facility for miles around. Aides who owed the home their LPN certification almost always stayed with the organization anyway, employment choices being what they were, and those who moved on to other for-profit facilities carried with them fond feelings and a distinct disinclination to do anything that might hurt the program.

You Don't Need to Recruit If They Never Leave

The whole area of employee management presents one of the starkest contrasts between entrepreneurial management and traditional nonprofit management, because the entrepreneurial non-profit executive's success makes for far more reasons for the average employee to stay on. Being truly entrepreneurial in employee management starts with recognizing that while good employees stay on the job for a variety of reasons, they only join for opportunity. The entrepreneurial nonprofit executive's job is to create the environment in which that opportunity can arise again and again and again for each individual employee.

A great deal of effort is routinely expended bemoaning the lack of a so-called career ladder in the nonprofit world. The absence of such a structure, it is said, leads to employee frustration and burnout.

Nonsense.

What leads to employee burnout is poor training in a stagnant environment. The very notion of a career ladder is a hierarchical idea almost completely foreign to the average nonprofit. To say that employees leave the field or get frustrated in it due to a lack of vertical movement ignores the three most important motivators in any professional situation: achievement, recognition, and the intrinsic rewards of the work itself. What the entrepreneurial nonprofit executive does, seemingly effortlessly, is to create a self-reinforcing connection among all of those elements to move the agency and its individual employees forward.

Often, the entrepreneurial nonprofit executive accomplishes this task by increasing the size of the agency. Indeed, it is because of this fact that he or she is often viewed with scorn and suspicion by outsiders, especially fellow executives. "Empire builder" and "egomaniac" are two of the nicer terms applied to the entrepreneurial executive creating opportunities for staff in this way, and it is true that growth in total agency revenue is often associated with the entrepreneurial nonprofit executive. But what outsiders sometimes don't understand is that what looks like growth for its own sake is really the organizational footprints of a series of mission-faithful efforts.

Cupid Had the Right Idea

A talent most entrepreneurial executives have that can actually be learned if it's not innate is the ability to match people with jobs.

I once redeemed a hiring decision of mine and created a long-term employee in the process by carefully fashioning a match between an employee's talents and work style and her job. It occurred to me that our new receptionist/secretary was extraordinarily methodical in the way she answered the phone. Unfortunately, her methodical style came across as coldness, and callers were beginning to take note.

When our bookkeeper quit and had to be replaced, I found myself wondering how our methodical front person would handle the job. So I asked her. It turns out that she had had a bit of accounting in the past, and, furthermore, she was tired enough of being tracked into receptionist jobs that she was willing to give bookkeeping a chance.

We set her up with a bit of outside help, signed her up for a bookkeeping course and gave her lots of support. Sure enough, she flourished. She had been planning to start an undergraduate program anyway and decided on a business major as a result of her new job. Today she's still there.

The very best entrepreneurial executives I've met seem to have an uncanny ability to judge employees' strengths and work styles and then bend jobs to fit them. If you have that skill, you probably already know it (do former employees refer to you with bliss in their eyes?), but the rest of us need to be a bit more calculating. Here is some help, based on the theory of conative employee management of a Phoenix-based former journalist and management consultant named Kathy Kolbe.

People, says Kolbe, are a blend of four distinct personality categories. The Fact Finder probes and analyzes thoroughly. The Follow Through loves charts and efficient systems and actually enjoys juggling the day-to-day details. Quick Starts take risks and act on hunches, and Implementors readily break a sweat getting the job done.[1]

Most of us are strong in one area, hit average in two, and are weak in the fourth. Naturally then, we structure things so as to avoid doing things the way we are weakest. That's fine if we're left to our own devices, but if the workplace in some way forces us to operate the way we are least comfortable it's a prescription for disaster.

Kolbe tells the story of a bank that made the mistake of putting Fact Finders, who had been spending their days rooting around the bank's systems as customer service representatives, into a Quick Start/cold call marketing role. The entire department eventually collapsed, because the new salespeople were still Fact Finders at heart and weren't bringing in new business.

The entrepreneurial nonprofit executive succeeds in this area because he or she deals only in strengths, as though a learning disability prevents the executive from seeing any employee weakness. As a positive driving force, this strategy is invaluable. It matches an employee's strong points with the nature of the work to be done, and it may even account for the uniquely personal nature of the executive's relationships with key employees often characteristic of the entrepreneur.

Incidentally, the practice of job rotation is gaining acceptance in management circles as a way of holding the line on employee turnover. For example, Florence Hesselbein, formerly of the Girl Scouts of America and now with the Drucker Foundation, has talked in recent years about the virtues of job swapping. She describes the benefits in an analogy using submarine command procedures, which have long recognized the personal and organizational virtues of training people in a variety of jobs.[2]

Conative employee management suggests that the right way to organize job swapping is with fastidious attention to preferred work styles. The energetic switchboard operator's move into the development office, for example, is more likely to be a productive switch than for the same person to become office manager, because the requirements for success in the first two jobs are much more similar.

Entrepreneurial management of employees capitalizes on the commitment to, or at least interest in, mission that is so natural to most people working in nonprofit organizations. By blending the opportunity to continually renew that commitment with careful attention to employee-job matching, the entrepreneurial executive creates momentum to carry forward the organization and its capacity to serve its mission.

CHAPTER 18

"... AND THOSE WHO CAN'T TEACH, CONSULT"

You almost have to pity the poor management consultant. He is laughed at ("Those who can, do; those who can't do, teach; those who can't teach, consult"); misunderstood (the IRS and assorted specialists put out reams of paper arguing about who is an employee and who is a consultant); and even attacked (one public employee union in Massachusetts actually spent two years and hundreds of thousands of dollars trying to prohibit state government from hiring consultants). Kids in high school never dream idly about the day when they can become management consultants and live happily ever after. Worse, ordinary salespeople have taken to calling themselves consultants, perhaps hoping that some additional fraction of the population will fail to see through the ruse.

On the other hand, graduates from the top-rank business schools continue to go into management consulting. Many of the top schools report that as much as a third of each graduating class goes into management consulting at average salaries of approximately seventy thousand dollars per year. A leading consultant newsletter—yes, they have their own newsletter—reports that the average in-house consultant earns eighty-eight thousand dollars, while a third earn over a hundred thousand. What's more, consulting is a growth industry. The U.S. Labor Department reports that management and consulting services are ninth on its list of ten small-business-dominated fields expected to grow the most during the coming decade: at a projected 379 percent growth rate (measured by number of jobs created), management consulting is right above legal services and right below computer services.

I said you *almost* have to pity the poor management consultant.

An Extremely Short History of Management Consulting

Management consulting as an identifiable profession began around the turn of the century in time-and-motion studies. The Industrial Revolution was in full swing, population shifts were just beginning to accommodate the new order, and Henry Ford was on the verge of paying his employees an unheard-of five dollars per day for producing the Model T. It must have seemed logical to have people with clipboards scouring the manufacturing process in minute detail for the sole purpose of squeezing further efficiencies from an already intricately engineered manufacturing flow. Several of today's best-known consulting firms—Arthur D. Little, Booz-Allen, and McKinsey—were founded during the first quarter of the century.

Today, the management consulting game is well over a tenbillion-dollar enterprise. Outside of the strategy houses such as Bain and the Boston Consulting Group, the newest major league entries into the ranks have been accounting firms. The largest six accounting firms alone account for four billion dollars in yearly revenue, and that compares favorably with their better-known audit practices. Not surprisingly, the bulk of accounting firms' management consulting work involves data processing and internal control systems, while strategy-oriented engagements go to the big-name organizations as well as regional ones. Throw in nonprofit consulting groups and fund raisers, technical assistance support centers, and associations' consulting to members, and you have a thoroughly eclectic group of consulting resources for the average nonprofit.

The Poles of Consulting

This is not a chapter devoted to persuading you to hire management consultants. If anything, it starts with the premise that you already do, or will, hire outside consultants. Many nonprofit organizations have traditionally been reluctant to hire so-called outsiders, ostensibly due to lack of funds, but perhaps due a little bit to a stubborn conviction that "we can do it just as well by ourselves."

Frankly, this is a tough attitude to change because it is the product of a severely limited executive vision. In today's complex society it is simply impossible, not to mention unwise, for any group to keep within itself the resources to meet every single challenge. So to say that everything can be handled from within is in effect saying that there are no complex challenges. The question of whether to hire management consultants is a little bit like the question of whether to convert from manual typewriters to electric: if you have yet to make the decision, it may be a sign of much more serious problems.

Incidentally, most nonprofit corporations already hire at least one or two consultants, even if that's not what they're called. The auditing firm that performs the yearly audit is a consultant in a broad sense of the term, and so is the lawyer who gives legal advice from time to time. It's only a small technical step to go from there to hiring more traditional kinds of consultants as well.

One of the things that makes the consultant hiring decision difficult is that there are so many contradictory yet perfectly valid ways it can be done. Let's look at a few.

Consultants versus consultants

There are only two kinds of consultants: Consultants, and consultants. Since both wear nice clothes, hand out good-looking business cards, and carry a briefcase, it's hard to tell them apart. To do that, you would have to look deep into their minds and psyches. If you can, you will see one difference: Consultants want to be doing this; consultants don't. Chances are the latter are simply specialists in between jobs doing consulting work temporarily or as a halfhearted attempt to build a small firm. Consultants with a capital C are presumably committed to consulting for the long haul—or at least some bona fide employer is committed to them.

There are advantages with either type. Short-term consultants can be a very good investment, provided that the task is suited to their skills and abilities. Professional consultants, however, offer the much harder to quantify advantage of depth and support. It is no accident that lawyers practice in groups, and that doctors increasingly are doing so. Engineers work best when in contact with other engineers, and you rarely find an accountant working completely alone.

What most professionals find useful about practicing in a group is that it creates synergies. If one need only walk down the hall to find an answer for a client, that answer will not only be more likely to be sought, but the dialogue about it might lead to some other discovery. The economic benefits of group practice are obvious too. Less obvious to the consumer is the self-regulating nature of professional group practices. Most professionals know a stiff when they see one, and if the stiff happens to be practicing from an office twenty paces away—well, there is an incentive to find ways of guiding him or her out of the practice before the damage spreads too far.

The Tyranny of the Billable Hour

One of the major differences between Consultants and consultants is the economics of their practices, and understanding those differences can give the entrepreneurial nonprofit executive a decided advantage in recruiting and hiring outside help.

Not unlike other providers of services—say, an auto mechanic, for example—the cost of paying the person who actually performs the service is only a fraction of the overall cost to the corporation selling the service. In addition to covering the employee's payroll costs, the organization must provide supplies and a physical setting for doing the job, as well as administrative support and some profit for the owner.

The biggest cost of consulting is not payroll or administration, however, it's downtime. Any consultant, no matter how efficient, needs to spend some portion of his or her time tending to routine administrative matters, researching the latest professional developments, and catching up on office gossip. No client can be billed for this time, yet it is an essential part of the job. The solution is to pick a certain number of hours per year as a target number to be billed to clients, and then to try to meet or exceed that number.

For consultants with some management or marketing responsibility, that number is often 60 percent of the working hours available each year, or approximately twelve hundred hours. Compensation costs in a professional services firm usually range from 30 to 45 percent of each dollar brought in. Therefore, the rate billed to clients is typically about three or more times the consultant's cost. Expressed another way, if you want to know your consultant's approximate annual salary (assuming he or she is also responsible for some firm administration and marketing), multiply his or her hourly billing rate by four hundred.

So far, we've only talked about the rate billed the consulting client, or the standard rate. Many other variables enter into the equation determining the actual rate, including things like unexpected expenses that the consultant cannot for some reason charge to the client, costs in excess of a preestablished cap, and nonpaying clients. Costs of this sort get charged directly to the consultant's project but without matching income they eat away at the standard rate. So the second number in which the consultant must be very interested is the percentage of the standard rate that actually got collected, or the realization (yield).

Armed with this knowledge, the entrepreneurial nonprofit executive can create a multitude of opportunities for his or her organization when it needs consulting services. The most powerful way to do this is to secure consulting services during a period that the consultant might otherwise have considered downtime. Exactly when that time might occur depends on many factors and differs from field to field.

Accounting firms, for example, increasingly find that the 1986 federal tax reform is causing for-profit clients to make their corporate tax year the calendar year, meaning that the number of audits to be done during that general period is rapidly increasing, while audits done at other times of the year, especially summer, are decreasing. Fund-raising consultants have their own special rhythm for mass mailing campaigns, and virtually any consulting organization would love to pick up some unexpected short-term business during the week between December 25 and January 1.

Many nonprofits, having made the decision to use consulting services, try to get them free. Before you wheel and deal around consulting services, however, consider that professional services in general are priced based on perceived value. The only quantifiable way of measuring any part of the transaction is by the amount of dollars that changed hands as a result of it. Therefore, the consultant inexperienced in nonprofit culture is liable to interpret your effort to get services for free as a commentary on what you think the services are worth.

If the organization is an association or otherwise well positioned to promise the consultant entry into a hitherto untapped market, soliciting a donation is a perfectly sensible approach. Shrewd consultants are always receptive to the chance to develop new sources of business even if it means doing a little pro bono work beforehand.

If your nonprofit is freestanding and only minimally connected to a large group of peers, there is a better alternative. Instead of asking for a donation of services—a tacky way to begin a relationship, if ever there was one—offer to cover the consultant's payroll. Offering to pay the 35 percent or so of standard costs that the payroll probably entails is a nice way of signaling respect for the consultant's services while still getting a wonderful deal. Go one step further by suggesting that the consultant actually record the balance as a donation, thereby benefiting from some tax relief. It's far from a surefire solution, but it is definitely worth the try.

Dealing with consultants is a very different ball game. Like their corporate counterparts, solo consultants also have overhead costs. Unlike them, the single practitioner almost always underestimates them. This drives his or her already low rate even lower, and makes the consultant look like the bargain that he or she is. At least, until the consultant realizes the mistake and starts trying to correct it.

The most important difference between a consultant and a Consultant is the nature of the work you want him or her to do. Largely out of necessity, a consultant offers a single skill or group of related skills that he or she uses over and over again. In truth, the dirty little secret behind many solo practitioners is that they do the same thing so often that it becomes, well, boring. Again, it is the economic imperative that makes this happen, most shrewd clients not being willing to knowingly subsidize a consultant's trip up a new learning curve.

In fact, the major rule in hiring a solo practitioner consultant is to remember that consulting is one thing that is definitely better the second time around. Ask if your prospective candidate has done this before. And don't be afraid to ask for references and to contact them if the answer is yes.

Few solo consultants are in a position to donate their services for very long. However, you can take advantage of the repetitive nature of some practices and of the consultant's possible boredom by structuring an engagement that is related to his or her prior work but just different enough to be intriguing. For some, the nonprofit connection alone is enough to break through the sameness barrier. While this does not necessarily mean a lower fee on paper, I have had consultants actually put in extra hours without charge just because the assignment was different enough to intrigue them.

Annuity versus Transaction

One of the major developments in professional services today, especially among consultants of various types, is that the relationship between consultant and client is moving from one of annuity to one of transaction. Here's what that means in English.

Technically, an annuity is defined as a payment made at regular intervals. Implicit in an annuity is that the payer and the payee have a relationship: at some point they sketched out the obligations of each, agreed to them, and then started the series of transactions. At the very least, they must still know how to get in touch with each other, and they may very well have an even closer relationship emcompassing other business.

Contrast this style with a transaction-oriented approach, in which the client engages the consultant for the purposes of a well-defined transaction. There is no previous history between the two, and the implicit understanding is that there may very well not be any future either (though not if the consultant has anything to say about it, of course). Or, the client may engage the consultant for a series of defined transactions over time, still with the expectation of a finite end point.

Since many nonmedical nonprofits only got to the point of using consultants during the shift to transaction-based business, this distinction may seem trivial. It's not. The methods and measures of success of a long-term relationship are very different from one based primarily on a single transaction.

To see the same evolution of a profession in stark terms, you need look no further than a service many nonprofit organizations provide, psychotherapy. Today psychotherapy is provided in outpatient settings heavily influenced by limitations on the amount insurers or government agencies are willing to pay. Inpatient hospitalization for psychotherapeutic purposes has also been effectively capped by funders, and therapists have turned to weekend sessions, small group sessions, and myriad time-limited approaches.

Sigmund Freud's notion of psychotherapy involved the psychotherapist seeing a handful of patients four or five days per week (out of a possible six) for years at a time. The very image of such a practice today seems wildly anachronistic, yet it was an accepted professional model not all that long ago.

What happened in psychotherapy, in fact, has occurred in virtually all of the professions, including medicine, law, and accounting. Transactions are the new basis of business, relationships—annuities—are secondary. Not surprisingly, the shift has meant that all types of professionals must spend more time marketing. More marketing means more nonbillable hours, but it also means that professionals who can find ways of reaching their intended market efficiently will be much in demand.

As always, there are opportunities for contrarian (read: entrepreneurial) nonprofit executives in industry trends. Essentially they involve bundling all of your consulting needs into a single package, if possible, then seeking out an explicitly long-term relationship with the right consultant. If you can do this, two good things will happen. First, your consultant should be amenable to dropping your per hour costs in return for the guaranteed business. (Why not? He stands to save on marketing costs.) Second, you will find yourself getting some special treatment. What this special treatment will amount to with any individual consultant will vary widely, but the consultant will likely do everything he or she can to enrich your own professional activities.

Will You Buy Time or Projects?

Another way to evaluate consulting service choices is the time versus project continuum. Ask yourself whether the task at hand requires a more or less finite number of additional person hours of the sort already provided by existing staff, or whether it is a separate project entirely. Obviously the difference will not always be clear-cut, but usually it will be workable.

Buying consulting services as additional versions of existing hours solves the problem of staffing for peak times and then carrying excess capacity during slack periods. This type of consultant also tends to be more commodity-like and therefore relatively lower level. Specialists in specific types of reports are a good example of extra-capacity consultants.

Project-oriented consultants initiate, plan, and/or carry out specific projects with a definable beginning and end. When the project stretches over a period of time, these consultants tend to resemble the annuity consultants talked about earlier. It is not a question of which kind is better or worse, but rather which one better suits the purposes of the engagement.

Strategy versus Tasks

A related distinction is the one between hiring consultants for specified tasks and hiring them for purposes of conceiving and carrying out strategy. Strictly speaking, strategy consulting is a subset of project consulting, though strategy is such a sweeping approach that it's hard to think of it as a type of project. "Tasks" as used here means something combining elements of both project and time. For example, an information system that relies on an out-of-house service bureau for routine processing uses a task-oriented consulting relationship. Fund-raising consulting can show the same elements. Unlike a project which has a beginning, middle, and end, task-focused consulting consists chiefly of the repeated performance of a defined procedure by outside specialists.

Strategy consulting is the glamorous corner of the consulting biz that is finding greater acceptance in the nonprofit world than ever before. Given the smaller size of most nonprofits compared to national and multinational corporations, strategy consulting is never likely to achieve the same level of intensity, acceptance, or prominence that it has among those who must worry about the next quarter's earnings report. Still, as nonprofits of all sizes face the effects of years of declining revenue streams, postponed operational and capital expenditures, and increasing demand for services, strategy consulting should grow geometrically as a primary long-term means of coping with the new complexities.

Experience versus Perspective

A final axis on which to evaluate consulting decisions is that of experience versus perspective. What is it, in other words, that you need to make the proper executive decision? To the unsophisticated buyer of consulting services, experience would seem to be the hands-down winner: bring in a graybeard and watch your problems melt away.

In my experience, knowledge of the field and longevity in it are important criteria for hiring a consultant, but they tend to function more as a screen than as a basis for hiring. That is, demonstrated experience and knowledge get the consultant in the door and keep him or her there but don't necessarily translate into success. What usually clinches the deal is the consultant's understanding of the role he or she is expected to play—the perspective with which the consultant must approach the job. Let's look over a few typical consultant roles:

Validator. Often those inside know exactly what needs to be done but do not have the status, reputation, or clout to articulate and then insist on it. Outside experts always seem to be possessed of a refreshing ability to settle on exactly the right course, especially if they have written a book on the subject. After about six or seven meetings, however, someone notices the dandruff on the consultant's shoulders and it's downhill from there. When the sheen of brilliance wears off, the consultant must rely on personal integrity and credibility to carry the rest of the job.

Lightning Rod. A step beyond validator is the consultant whose major job is to recommend an unpopular course of action and then absorb the outrage so that management can go about making it work without being directly attacked.

Scapegoat. Enough said, except that it's a rare consultant who will knowingly enter into a relationship like this one.

Delayer. A sophisticated use of consultants, this game pretends to be advancing a particular cause through a flurry of activity, while in reality there is no movement at all. It requires a smart, likable but naive consultant and a Machiavellian employer, and it can be good for two or three years.

Agent. Nothing more than the consultant's agreement to act in lieu of the employer while maintaining a clearly independent stance. Good for creating distance between employer and the action.

Talisman. Employers hire talismans in the hopes that their long experience, in-depth knowledge, and wide respect will rub off due to sheer proximity.

Consultant Ethics

As the term "consultant" comes to mean anything from a post-doctoral Egyptology specialist to a cosmetics salesperson in disguise, the entrepreneurial nonprofit executive will carefully and closely review all consulting relationships. High on the list for review, right after competence and price, should be consulting ethics.

By their nature, certain types of consulting engagements make the consultant privy to extremely confidential information. Yet most of the time there are no explicit laws or regulations to stop the consultant from using that information for narrow personal gain. What will stop him or her is a strong code of ethics.

The consulting profession has no licensors, regulators, or gatekeepers and probably never will. While this state of affairs has many benefits for consultants and clients alike, it does not provide for any self-policing. This is what a code of ethics will supply.

Large national firms, especially fund raisers, will maintain their own code of ethics and will very likely give you a copy on request. Others may belong to the Institute of Management Consultants, a leading industry group with high standards and higher expectations of the profession. The IMC's intention is to improve the practice of management consulting and the public's perception of it. Even if your consultant does not belong to the IMC, he or she ought to have a code of ethics available for you, and this document is a good guide to what you want to hear.

Management consultants can mean more to a nonprofit organization than being the butt for a few stale jokes. The field as a whole is growing, and many practitioners either focus on nonprofits or are intrigued by them. The wise entrepreneurial nonprofit executive knows how and when to take advantage of that interest.

CHAPTER 19

THE DYING ART OF IGNORING LEGAL ADVICE

You pay a lawyer to do one thing and one thing only: keep you and your organization out of trouble. You, on the other hand, are paid to know when to ignore your lawyer.

Nothing can tie a nonprofit executive into knots faster than bad legal advice. Lawyers are essentially analysts. By necessity they must spend most of their intellectual energy looking backward at cases and at that codified system of prescribed behaviors called the law. They can tell you with often exquisite precision what your predecessors did under similar circumstances, and they can suggest a general course of action to embrace or avoid, but that's it. Your lawyer may be a wonderful planner, a leader, or even a visionary, but if he or she is, consider it a bonus.

In seeking a guide through legal labyrinths the natural urge is to find a compatible soul and stick with him or her. Don't do it. Legal matters aren't that simple. You actually need as many as three different kinds of lawyers, depending on the type and complexity of your project. It would be a lot easier if lawyers were horses. If they were, the three major types would look like this:

Quarter Horses

These are the lawyers suited for everyday needs. They can sprint or carry loads a short distance. They're not glamorous, but they get the job done with a minimum of fuss. Use them for routine transactions, like purchasing a building or reviewing a lease. The

205

great majority of the transactions carried out by the average nonprofit agency don't require any special knowledge of nonprofit organizations or even any particularly deep knowledge of a specialized field of law. So why pay for what you don't need?

The quarter horse lawyer is best used for transactions. The role is largely technical, and in fact you may discover that, in the case of a quarter horse firm, the bulk of the actual work is done by paralegals or law students. No cause for alarm here: most nonattorneys don't appreciate the routine nature of much legal work.

Quarter horse lawyers are the type most often found on community-oriented nonprofits' boards. Like their counterparts, they too are specialized. The difference is that they tend to specialize by function—real estate transactions, wills and trusts, etc.—rather than by an area of interest or type of business.

Quarter horses are also the most dangerous of the three types of lawyers because they are far more common and therefore are more likely to be within easy reach when you feel a legal itch coming on. You'll be able to tell when you've found a good quarter horse by the number of times that he tells you he just doesn't know enough about that type of law to be helpful. No advice is better than bad advice.

Finding a good quarter horse attorney should be relatively easy. Most of the names board members, staff, and others suggest will tend to be quarter horses, if only because that's the most common type of attorney around. Although the attorney's knowledge is important, of course, what's more important is your relationship. Comfort with your organization's size and working style are the key factors here.

Thoroughbreds

These are highly trained, highly specialized lawyers who, with a little bit of luck, most nonprofits will only need to hire once in a while. You should hire them for their experience and judgment, not their technical expertise, which is likely to be no better than anyone else's and is almost certain to be more expensive. They are elegantly prepared, thoroughly knowledgeable experts on a specific area of law.

Like quarter horses, thoroughbreds tend to cut across industries, which is why the thoroughbred you hire today will spend tomorrow handling a case involving a tire dealer. Unlike the quarter horse, however, thoroughbreds concentrate deeply on a single area of the law rather than trying to master a bunch of often-repeated legal services. I have known thoroughbreds specializing in everything from labor relations to tax law. One thoroughbred attorney I know spent the better part of ten years concentrating on nothing but cases involving zoning laws, and at the end of that time he had racked up a string of precedent-setting cases.

Hire a thoroughbred when you need the intangible boost that a purist's dedication can bring. Chances are the thoroughbred has a mission—to fight for the little guy against government tax lawyers, to improve the collective bargaining process—and if your situation falls within that mission you'll be in line for some really high-powered advice.

Thoroughbreds tend to be found in medium to large-sized law firms or working as lone eagles for the simple reason that they need either a large overhead and a ton of supporting specialists or the freedom to devote just about all of their time and money to their interest. For obvious reasons they are likely to be the most costly of the three types of attorneys you'll need. At the same time, you'll only be using them when the stakes are so high that anything less than first-rate help is pointless anyway.

With such a large portion of your yearly budget going toward employees, the laws of probability alone suggest that most of the thoroughbred help you'll need will be related to labor or tax law. It's not a bad idea to keep the names of one or two such types on file just in case you need one in a hurry.

Clydesdales

Clydesdale lawyers are the beasts of burden for nonprofit organizations. They are made for carrying heavy legal and pseudolegal loads. They're impressive at any distance, but they're definitely not built for speed or economy. The hallmark of Clydesdale lawyers is that they are almost always the creature of a funding source, government or otherwise. They are denizens of their own specialized world, often a world partly of their own creation. They are former government regulators and auditors, ex-foundation presidents, former politicians. They build their practice around a special need connected in some way with nonprofit organizations, and often they are one-of-a-kind. One attorney I know spent a few years with a state attorney general as a public charities lawyer, then developed a sort of dime-in-the-washing-machine practice based on finding money that nonprofits had had donated to them but had forgotten to claim or couldn't use anymore because of obsolete restrictions in the original bequest.

Clydesdales talk your language. They know your business better than either the quarter horse or thoroughbred, and the chances are good that your paths have crossed before or will cross again. They are the lawyers who help you put together the five-hundred-page government funding application, the complex foundation proposal, the innovative multiple-agency consortium. What you are really hiring with a Clydesdale is an intricate web of personal connections and knowledge, and the understanding of obscure processes that your organization may go through only once or twice. Don't dismiss the Clydesdale as an out-of-office politician, for two reasons: one, even an old politician can be useful; and two, it's never that simple anyway. Clydesdales have a role in your legal strategy.

How to Buy Legal Services

The market for legal services is regional. The biggest name in Anaheim means nothing in Allentown and vice versa. So, unlike public accounting, where a handful of big-name firms dominate the market, legal work is shaped and evaluated by local demand. What this means in practice for the entrepreneurial nonprofit manager is that the don't-worry-we've-got-the-best-talent-working-for-us effect that comes from hiring a national household name firm will never be realized. That being the case, the manager has a fair degree of latitude in shopping for legal counsel. Take advantage of it.

What makes lawyers really dangerous for the conventional nonprofit manager has more to do with the managers than the lawyers themselves, and it's that old Something for Nothing attitude. This is dangerous because one of the easiest things to get is free legal advice, yet the entrepreneurial nonprofit manager knows that free legal advice is worth exactly what you pay for it. The plain reality is that an exchange of money for advice tends to keep both parties focused and alert.

If you simply must stay in the old mode when it comes to legal dealings, turn free legal advice into free legal *teaching*. Lawyers instinctively concentrate on individual cases and specific laws. That's natural, because they already understand what links often wildly different cases and laws together. You don't, or you wouldn't be hiring a lawyer. Instead of getting bogged down in the details of your case, insist that your attorney lay out the broad underlying principles of the law. This solves the problem of the moment while preparing you to think your way through the next one. Two for the price of one, and about as close as you should allow yourself to get to the Something for Nothing approach.

Better still, have your lawyer do the same kind of work with the administrative and managerial staff. Chances are that the staff will be less entrepreneurially inclined than senior management, so the trick here is for the lawyer to spend a lot of time granting "permission" to do what they were worried they couldn't do.

One word of caution if you do plan to expose your staff to legal teaching: make it a strict and explicit condition of the agreement that the lawyer be absolutely forbidden from telling even a single horror story. Seriously. The difference between ordinary case law and horror stories is that the latter are usually unique cases that in some way break new legal ground or threaten to overturn some principle previously taken for granted. They may or may not be harbingers of things to come, but either way they mean far more to connoisseurs of the law than they do to ordinary people who just need to know the basics.

The wisest thing a nonprofit manager can do both to hold down costs and maintain management prerogatives is always to frame problems as management choices needing legal guidance, not legal dilemmas needing legal resolutions. One director of a medium-sized nonprofit I knew had four lawyers on his board of directors. This was the single largest concentration of professional expertise among the directors, and in fact many of the rest of the board were not professionals of any sort. Having only a hammer, this group's problems all tended to look like nails, with the result that the poor director was routinely whipsawed back and forth among the four legal specialties represented, and most of their collectively decided actions had a legal hue to them.

Many nonprofits are concerned about the cost of legal advice, and for good reason. While you need to be prepared to pay a substantial amount of money for extended legal work, there are things you can do. For one, ask your lawyer if she offers a nonprofit discount. Also, consider bartering for legal work.

There is one exception to the prohibition against free legal advice, though it most often comes after you've paid for some. The way to get it is simple and pleasant: invite a Clydesdale to lunch. A long lunch with the right Clydesdale can be worth more than a week's worth of convention-going. The Clydesdale attorney's stock in trade comes from his or her dealings with dozens of people in your position and dozens if not hundreds of others whose work touches you and your organization in some way. Forcing yourself to ask one detailed but interesting question after another without saying much yourself will give you far more information about general trends and conditions in your organization's environment than you could possibly obtain on your own.

If you're really worried about cost, nothing works better than carefully managing your use of legal resources. For example, make it a policy to confer with your attorney only in his or her own office. For these purposes, the farther away the office is or the harder it is to reach it, the better. Then, prepare for each session as though it were a cross between a coronation and the Spanish Inquisition. Study the question thoroughly ahead of time, and exchange as much correspondence as necessary. By the time you get into the actual meeting many questions will seem to answer themselves and you'll get to the ones that don't faster. More important, you won't need to repeat the experience as often.

Alternative Dispute Resolution

One of the most interesting developments in the legal field is the rise of alternatives to traditional legal methods of resolving conflicts. Lumped under the descriptive if inelegant term, alternative dispute resolution (ADR), these methods range from the very simple and inexpensive to the complex and costly. What they all have in common is that they represent a way of privately resolving disputes that can also be faster and cheaper than prolonged litigation.

Occupational injury cases, particularly asbestos-related claims, are one of the prime areas for ADR because it offers a way of processing thousands of individual cases sharing very similar features without bogging down the court system. Our legal system was built on the premise that court appearances would be unique, customized affairs, so traditional legal routes don't usually offer the operational nimbleness necessary for disposing of huge numbers of cases. Alternative dispute resolution can be used as a legal and mutually acceptable substitute.

Few nonprofit organizations are likely to be involved in mass injury cases, but ADR might be useful in more mundane matters. For instance, I know of a group trying to locate a group home in a resistant neighborhood that used ADR with success. It could pay to have an ADR capacity lined up if an organization senses it is venturing into tumultuous waters, and ADR is certainly an option for internal disputes that just can't seem to get settled through traditional routes.

Being fleet of foot in legal affairs is more essential for any chief executive officer now than it ever has been, and there is every reason to expect that it will continue that way. The entrepreneurial nonprofit executive needs to stay out of trouble as much as everyone else. He or she just knows how to do it faster and less expensively.

CHAPTER 20

SHAPE THE COMPUTER, NOT THE PEOPLE

There are only two good reasons to buy a computer. One is to be able to do what you are already doing faster and, presumably, better. The other is to change what you are doing. Therein lies the substance of several good books. We'll try to cover the topic in a short chapter.

Twenty or so years ago, when computers first began to touch the average person's life, they were employed to carry out complex everyday tasks faster and better. Things like getting invoices out on time, meeting payroll, and processing minor financial data were a natural area for the first computers to target. Eventually, they—we—learned how to do these things well. Extremely well, in fact. This is partly what accounted for the seeming explosion in the use of massive computer systems, and for our sense as consumers of being swept forward on a wave of unprecedented technological innovation.

The early systems—and today's simple ones—are very good at making mundane but time-consuming jobs routine. Paul Strassman, an information strategist and consultant whose ideas permeate this chapter, calls this function *acceleration* and says that using the computer as a machine tool to automate repetitive office work helps make savings because it cuts down the expense of structured office work, which can be as much as 30 percent of the cost of handling information.

There are two ways to create opportunity here using computers. The first is simply to begin using computers if you haven't

213

already. Since most agencies, even small ones, already use computers for generic tasks such as word processing this area has probably been plumbed for any given agency. Still, it should not be taken for granted. Perhaps, for example, there are generic functions that have escaped computerization. This is the chance for opportunity creation.

The second area is wide open for innovation, and it consists of making routine computerized operations out of previously overlooked processes. I ran into just such an opportunity when my first child was born and I went looking for a licensed day-care arrangement for him. A state agency sponsored a day-care provider/parent matching service, and the helpful worker who answered my call spent a great deal of time lovingly matching me up with half a dozen eligible providers.

Midway through our second conversation (which occurred after a week's worth of telephone tag and an exchange of correspondence), it occurred to me that what she was doing could have been handled equally as well with the careful use of a telephone answering machine and a relatively modest computer database. The inefficiency must have occurred to the legislature too; four years later, it closed the agency down.

As nonprofits feel revenue squeezes more in the future, computerizing functions formerly done by human beings represents one of the few ways to increase productivity. Yes, it will ruffle feathers among the purists on staff, but change usually does. It's an innovation worth making.

Microchip as Change Agent

The second reason for buying a computer system is to fundamentally change the way you do what you do—transformation, if you will. If acceleration is essentially a matter of figuring out a match between technology and task, transformation is the process of altering task altogether. What makes the effort so difficult is that the nature and extent of the change are intimately linked to the technology.

The first computer filled a large room and performed calculations on a par with today's hand calculators. Early commercial applications were variations on this single theme, and by the time of what we think of as the computer revolution the model was firmly in place: a massive central unit around which revolved a number of users. This was the mainframe computer, a behemoth adapted to any type of business or government activity as long as it was *big*.

The advent of the personal computer in the late 1970s seemed to change all that. It made a chunk of that enormous computational power available to those of us who didn't know a mainframe from a mainsail. Now it was possible to put a PC on one's desk and harness the same kind of analytical magic that the mainframes routinely provided. IBM's introduction of its PC in 1981, followed by a never-ending series of clones, appeared to make computing available to the masses.

In fact, the PC did just that. But for all its power, the personal computer alone was never more than a miniature version of its mainframe ancestor. Even some of the terminology reinforced the early PCs' identity as a shrunken version of the real thing. It was, after all, a *micro*computer. The section where computing actually took place was still called the central processing unit (central to what—itself?). And so on. In the end, the PC stand-alone was only as powerful as the input each user arranged for it to receive.

Beginning in the late 1980s the real promise of personal computing began to be routinely harnessed by networked PCs. By parceling out specialized segments of work in the processing of information to specializing machines—called servers—a network of personal computers does the same thing as a mainframe but does so faster, cheaper, with more flexibility and greater power than the do-it-all mainframe.

Strassman says that the history of business has really been about the breakup of successive monopolies, beginning with the monopoly on land in the Middle Ages. The next monopoly to be broken is the one on knowledge, currently held by big bureaucracies in business, government, and universities. In due time, what is now specialized knowledge will be turned into a commodity to be bought and sold along with everything else. Rather than people being specialists, the specialization will come in the form of products and services, and the people will be generalists. The personal computer network is nothing more than a small step in that direction.

That antimonopoly power—or, if you prefer, the mass empowerment effect—of the personal computer network is what gives it its organizational potency. Now I can reach into your environment, and you can reach into mine. Total distance from top to bottom in any organization shrinks when top and bottom have access to the same information and the same tools to process it. The power to accomplish this resides in the network itself, not in any one machine or specialist.

This is why computerization, done properly, utterly transforms any organization. Even a single PC in a small agency will transform it, but a carefully designed network will vault the host organization forward in time. It moves the agency into a completely different managerial dimension by reducing the amount of time spent on purely technical matters and elevating the focus of more of the administrative work to the conceptual level. Managers can then spend more of their time considering the effectiveness of the system itself, rather than why a handwritten spreadsheet won't balance.

There is another way in which computers, especially networked computers, transform an organization. When an organization is small, one person in the executive role can carry around everything important in his or her head. At some point in an organization's growth, however, that has to change. Eventually, the executive's major information-disseminating role shifts from directing and specifying to coordinating. Later on, much of that coordinating role starts to be taken up by meetings and ad hoc groups. Allowed to continue long enough, this process takes on a life of its own and additional staff need to be added to cope with what seems like a crushing work load but in reality is mainly a system of coordinators coordinating coordinators.

Computerizing the agency intelligently helps avoid coordinator buildup by spreading information access over a large number of people. This is more of a necessity in the nonprofit sector than it might appear, since tradition and grant gamesmanship often lead to coordinators whose job is to coordinate other coordinators and who end up acting like a shadow administration. By speeding the flow of information around an organization, computers reduce overhead, or at least shrink the rate at which overhead needs to grow.

The Computer Decision

The decision to purchase a computer system as it is usually construed—the software and the hardware—is actually the tail end of a very long process that has very little to do with technology and everything to do with people's minds. If the entire process of selecting and installing a computer system were laid out in chronological order and weighted according to its percentage of importance, the steps would look like this:

Change People's Minds (70 percent)

Draw a line across the American population at age forty. The farther down in age you go from that line, the more likely you are to find people comfortable with computers. The farther up in age you go, the less comfort you will find. The less personal familiarity with computers people have, the less likely they are to accept computerization from the beginning. More important, the less professional security people have, the more they are likely to resist computers either sweetly ("Oh, no, you don't have to spend all that money on *me*.") or otherwise ("The day you put one of those things on my desk is the day I quit.").

The reason for this can often be found in the special nature of nonprofit administrative hiring patterns. To get the maximum combination of knowledge for low salary, executives will sometimes hire the experienced middle-aged worker. Often these people have lots of personal experience; their knowledge has been won piece by hard-earned piece. But without an understanding of the underlying principles of finance and administration, as soon as they are in a situation that has no counterpart in their experience—such as computerization—they founder.

The response is to offer deep and unqualified support as the transition to computers begin. Try this twist for the truly terrified. Six months or so before the first computers arrive, buy one of the most attractive, user-friendly, full-color versions of the computer line you expect to purchase eventually and put it in some easily accessible place with a handful of irresistible software games. By the time the serious stuff arrives everyone in the office will be quite comfortable with computers, as well as being video game junkies.

The defiantly computer illiterate backroom people are most troublesome. Don't mistake this breed for the terrified variety. Their resistance to computers stems from a desire to keep things firmly under control—*their* control. Your pushing ahead with computerization opens a contest of raw power, however diplomatically it may be carried out, and unhappily there usually isn't much alternative to complete victory for one side. Let that side be yours or you'll never computerize successfully in this century.

The biggest people challenge from computers, however, especially in small agencies, is that they begin to create a demand for computer knowledge inside the agency. As long as two or more people have the inclination to get and maintain that knowledge you'll be okay. But ignoring the necessity for someone to become the in-house computer guru is asking for trouble.

Select the Software (20 percent)

Far more important than kicking the tires on a few racy computers—we'll get to that in a minute—is figuring out what you actually want the system to do that isn't being done now or that needs to be done faster. It may sound trite, but the first step in the software process is to decide if what it is you want to do really is done best by a computer. Strassman says that most computer systems are bought essentially on faith, and he's right. In the end, there is practically no way to apply cold, hard, analytical judgments to the decision to purchase one computer system or another.

I once worked with a methadone maintenance clinic that wanted to computerize its dispensing area to speed up processing times and reduce the number of addicts congregating in the hallway and outside the door. When we looked more deeply into the situation we discovered that they were right—computerization could save them time in the dispensing area, but mainly at the back end when the dispensary was closed and the nurses laboriously and often incorrectly added up their records.

The real source of the delay was in the mixing of the medicine, strictly governed by state laws and therefore less susceptible to time savings, and in the physical layout of the place. Computerizing the process had its advantages, and in fact that is exactly what they ended up doing later on, but the identified problem was caused by situations outside the reach of the ordinary computer.

Searching for software for a nongeneric application (if all you need is Lotus 1-2-3, buy on price) can be one of the most pleasant and educational experiences you'll have, especially if the vendors you call have toll-free numbers. They are usually more than happy to talk about their package, and comparing the various approaches can teach you a lot. This is one area where the traditional three-bids-and-buy approach is a must, not because it will result in the lowest price but because it will result in the overall best package.

Now buy the Hardware (10 percent)

By the time you have prepared the staff and selected the software, the hardware decision is anticlimactic. Most of the hard questions already have been answered, and specifying the hardware becomes chiefly a matter of meeting the software's minimum requirements with whatever combination of features is desirable. If you can put this step off until the end you'll find your computerization will truly be an entrepreneurial experience.

Twenty years from now, when computerphobia is a thing of the past and the average worker is as familiar with a computer as with a microwave, it will seem to be belaboring the obvious to talk about computers as entrepreneurial tools. For now, however, getting at least one is one of the smartest decisions the visionary executive can make.

CHAPTER 21

USING THE MEDIA

Movies about reporters should be outlawed. Most reporters I know don't smoke cigars, drink Jack Daniels, look like Dustin Hoffman, or have three months to pour into an obscure investigation of a murder no one else cares about. In fact, most local reporters I've known shop at Kmart, can't get good day-care for their kid, and when they get a faraway look in their eyes in the middle of an interview it's not because of a sudden flash of insight but because they're wondering whether their car will be towed or just ticketed again.

The first step you can take toward using the media in your agency's interests is to get rid of your media-as-monolith attitude. You know the feeling. It's the vague sense that if the phone on Peter Jennings's desk rings, maybe, just maybe, the voice on the other end will be the local television police reporter, and that the two will be on a first-name basis. This common perception, not always discouraged by the media itself, is responsible for keeping many nonprofit media stars from ever rising.

Instead of being a well-oiled machine, the media is actually a vast commodity distribution system. Except that instead of commodities, the product being distributed is abstract and intangible. To get to the heart of what the media do, think about how fresh fruits and vegetables reach your table. All over the country there are hundreds of thousands of growers producing hundreds of varieties of fruits and vegetables. Regionally based buyers pick them up and make the first decisions about price, quality, and likely consumers.

221

From there they go into national and even international distribution, ending up once again at local or regional markets for final passage to retail outlets and then on to your table. In most cases only a few days elapse from the time the fruits or vegetables leave the vine until they arrive at your house. They probably travel a great distance but in many cases pass through various hands without even being actually seen.

This is a fair analogy to the system of news distribution into which entrepreneurial nonprofit executives need to break. My cousin once did so without the slightest intention of getting press coverage, and her story illustrates how the media really work.

A guidance counselor in a northern Vermont town, she became intrigued with the situation of one of her students, a Cambodian refugee. The teenager had reason to believe that his mother and sister, held at one point by the Khmer Rouge, were still alive. He was determined to find them, and asked his teachers for help. After a short time, his quest became the high school's cause. The students wrote to their congressman and senator, the State Department, and Cambodia itself. They telephoned anyone they thought might possibly be helpful and held fund raisers to cover the costs.

Along the way the local paper picked up the story. From there the largest paper in the state got interested. At one point the *New York Times* ran the story in one of its weekday editions. That's undoubtedly what tipped off the network, which sent a camera crew to film the successful reunion. Not to be outdone by their network counterparts, Boston television stations also went to the airport—and put their version of the story on the air a half-hour before that night's network telecast.

If the news media are a distribution system in disguise, then it's only slightly stretching the metaphor to see reporters as entrepreneurs with notepads. A media outlet of just about any kind has a ferocious appetite for stories, and the people who feed it are its reporters. In effect, they are "selling" their stories to their editors, even if those same editors assigned or at least authorized pursuit of the stories in the first place, and even if the budget is too small to allow much latitude to reject completed stories. The entrepreneurial nonprofit executive takes advantage of this situation by thinking like a reporter.

A reality of today's world is that the average nonprofit executive will have at least some extended contact with one or more branches of the media during his or her career. The only real question is not whether it will happen but when, and whether it will be voluntary or involuntary. Fortunately there is a great deal that the executive can do to help insure a favorable outcome even if the contact is uninvited. Let's get that part out of the way before considering more positive and constructive ways to use the media.

What to do When a Mr. Wallace of CBS News Is Waiting For You in the Lobby (Defensive Media Strategies)

Okay, so maybe the vast majority of nonprofit executives never need to worry about Mike Wallace snooping around their program. But there is a real possibility that some Monday morning will find the local publisher's twenty-five-year-old journalism school graduate son sitting in your waiting room because he thinks he's on to a hot one involving your agency. You will wonder what he's doing there. Don't waste time speculating. Any reporter from any type of media has only one reason for seeking out you or your program—he or she wants you to be a character in a morality play. Morality plays were popular in the fifteenth and sixteenth century when they acted out common moral dilemmas using characters that epitomized some basic element of human life such as Love, Friendship, Death, etc. We may have come a long way since then in the technology of our media, but for the most part the reporters that nonprofit executives are likely to see are still acting out morality plays. The only blank spaces are the details of the particular play, and which character you are expected to be. The first answer you can find out right away, the second may take some time and a little careful inquiry.

Here is one area where having the kind of large bureaucracy and specialized staffing that many nonprofit executives instinctively reject could actually be an enormous benefit. With a bit of luck and an adequate public relations department, the would-be executive/target can completely avoid direct contact with inquiring reporter types, delegating the job instead to an aide of choice. In addition to buffering the manager, this move has the dual advantages of depersonalizing the conflict and being a weird kind of efficiency: public relations types tend to speak reporters' lingo, know some mutual colleagues, and even hang out in the same haunts. They don't need to spend much time Getting to Know Each Other because figuratively, if not literally, they already do. Plus, never underestimate the value of delegating conflict to a surrogate.

If you have no press department to call on, you are on your own. Very quickly you will know—if you don't already suspect— whether the role envisioned for you is Good Guy or Bad Guy. If the reporter signals that you are the former, your biggest problem will be to figure out how much you want to say that might get other less good guys in trouble.

On the other hand, if you are expected to be the Bad Guy in this production, you actually have two problems. Most reporters don't go looking for stories in nonprofit organizations, so by the time a reporter suspects that you or your agency are guilty of something, it is really a double indictment: guilty of the alleged acts and guilty of being a nonprofit (read: morally superior) agency carrying out the alleged acts. This produces the delicious aroma of festering hypocrisy, which for a good reporter is better than the smell of freshly brewed coffee in the morning.

Even if you are the designated Bad Guy; do not panic. Listen carefully to what the reporter has to say as he or she frames questions, and be ready to ask a few of your own. Draw the reporter out about the background of the story—what he or she has learned so far, from whom, and his or her interpretation of it. Do it gently, though, because most reporters are keenly sensitive to being the recipient of tough questions rather than the asker. A good way of doing this is to coax the reporter into asking the question a different way: "I'm not sure what you mean by 'clear-cut negligence.' Can you give me an example?" You can also rephrase the question yourself: "Are you asking if the security guard on duty that night was sleeping on the job?"

Also, the reporter may unwittingly help you understand the theme he or she is building. Less skilled reporters will often ask questions that are really restatements of fact as they see it, so you can garner a lot of information just from the wording of the questions.

With luck, this initial step may give you enough information to stop the process dead in its tracks. The best thing that could happen is for the reporter to be working from bad information—not just minor factual inaccuracies, but absolute, unequivocal, plain-as-the-nose-on-your-face errors. If that's the case, you can hit a home run by proving the mistakes. Just be sure you let the reporter save face ("of course, you had no way of knowing this"), because the last thing you need is a reporter looking for a second chance to prove what a jerk you are.

That part about hitting the home run? Make that a triple. Because the simple fact that a story is ill-conceived or just plain wrong never guarantees it will be killed. For whatever reasons, the thing may still run in its original or near-original form. If that happens there is little you can do about it, but at least you have a ready-made rebuttal for quick release.

If you have stayed calm, analyzed the reporter's preconceptions, and looked unsuccessfully for material flaws in the allegations, you have only one option remaining. At this point you must become a Concerned Fiduciary. Call for an investigation, vow to get to the bottom, etc. In doing so you grab the moral high ground back from the reporter, who is always presumed to be working from said lofty perch. You tend to break the momentum of the story and turn the accusations back into something you can use to your own advantage. And of course, you may actually learn what really went on and be in a good position to do something about it.

Understand that this is not merely a nice thing to do—at this stage it is the *only* thing you can do. One director of a social service agency I know was asked by a local reporter who had done her homework for a response to allegations that one of his agency's staff members had raped a client. He responded with a single word guaranteed never to be printed in any local newspaper. Within a month the story was way out of control, occupying a special place in several issues of the newspaper over the next few weeks. Within a year the director had found other employment. Very distressing, especially when the highly visible appointment of a special investigative task force, commission, or some other such device could have prevented the whole affair.

The key to what I call the Concerned Fiduciary strategy is distance. You already have a great deal of distance between yourself and the alleged impropriety just because you were not actually present when it supposedly occurred (you weren't, were you?). You need to use every bit of that distance now, and for two reasons. First, it buys you time. It's not likely, but it is possible that the whole thing will blow over without your having to do anything else. Reporters can be like little news machine mechanics, and if it takes an extra special amount of persistence to get your particular machine up and running against your will—well, there are easier machines waiting to be started up.

The second reason for using the Concerned Fiduciary strategy is that it also gives you the opportunity to gain control of the story. Much news reporting is profoundly analytical and passive because so much is tied up in background research. As long as the reporter is in that stage, there is no story. In the absence of any public airing, the matter is strictly between you, the reporters/ editors, and whoever else is directly involved in the story. This gives you the chance to reframe the reporters' thinking ("All the literature suggests that security guards are superior to mechanical alarm systems for our purposes. Why are you challenging that principle?"), bring up new facts, and even use other types of media to position your agency more favorably in the event that the story does come out.

A negative piece of publicity is like ringing the fire alarm in a grammar school: false alarm or the real thing, the only thing that will save you is lots of structure and a few practice runs ahead of time. Even for a disciplined, seasoned organization, a negative story in the media can be a chaotic event. Usually it's impossible to gauge how damaging the story is, so it's essential that you check your first impressions with knowledgeable outsiders who have the perspective to be a bit more clearheaded.

In the first few hours after a story hits is the time for damage assessment, a practice drawing far more deeply from art than science. In fact, "art" may be overstating the case; "groping" is more like it. It isn't pretty, but there is no substitute for groping your way around to find out the true extent of damage. Call people inside the organization and outside. Call a board member. Call your Aunt Gert. Call anyone you can think of to help you get some perspective on how this story is being interpreted. It may take some time, but in the end it will be worth it.

This is also the time when you decide whether to issue a response of any kind, or whether to let the story sink of its own presumed weight. If Governor Michael Dukakis's ill-fated presidential campaign did nothing else, it should have persuaded the few remaining skeptics that it is almost always better to rebut negative stories than to leave them unchallenged. The hard question is the nature and intensity of the rebuttal.

See No Evil, Hear No Evil, Speak No Evil, and You'll Never Be on the Six O'Clock News (Offensive Media Strategies)

Fortunately, the media exist for more than simply making your life miserable. Once you understand how the media work, you can use them as one more tool in your toolbox, whether for a single project or ongoing public relations. To set the foundation for any kind of effective work with the media, you need only do one thing: *give 'em conflict*. There are three types of conflict: person against person, person against a superior force, and person against nature. Let's take them one at a time.

Person against person is the easiest and most popular type of conflict for the media to cover. Murders, street crime, and civil disputes are all examples of person-against-person conflict. This is also the least promising category of conflict for you to push for your agency. Even if you could find a way to frame a conflict involving your agency as person to person, you'd be liable to get slimed in the process if the underlying conflict blew up. Avoid it if you can.

Person against a superior force is much better. When I lobbied for nonprofit organizations I used this one liberally since it was easy to paint a single nonprofit group—or even the entire nonprofit field—as a David against virtually any Goliath I chose.

Person against nature is nice too, in carefully defined situations. Usually this relates to physical or mental disability. These are the stories about individual courage in overcoming handicaps and the congregation that rebuilds a church destroyed by fire.

Framing the whole thing as a conflict is only half of your job. The other half is getting the reporter and his or her readers to take your side, preferably without realizing it. Given the circumstances this shouldn't be too hard, but don't just assume it will happen. What you're looking for is instant credibility. Catholic priests have it in spades, as long as they wear collars. Nuns are great too, especially if you can find a feisty one with gray hair. Anyone in a wheelchair is likely to be terrific. (A wheelchair-bound friend of my wife's used to make a practice of picketing movie theaters on Saturday night with other people in chairs, demanding that the theaters make themselves accessible to handicapped people. Watching the theater manager make his sweaty-lipped way through a response on the eleven o'clock news after a night of wheelchair picketing always seemed downright sadistic.) Once you have the conflict angle secured, it's time to start thinking about media strategies. Here are some proven ones.

Stage an Event

Try this test. Look at your smallest local newspaper, the one that costs a quarter or so and gets mailed to your home once each week. Add up the number of front-page articles that came out of something that had been previously scheduled. Chances are you'll find that at least 80 percent of the stories—or the events that created the stories—were planned by someone. You'll find the same kind of thing on local television and radio stations too. So-called late-breaking news doesn't exist for these outlets because they can't afford it. Scheduled news events are easier to manage, so they allow the outlet to get by with fewer reporters.

The best kind of scheduled event is a government meeting related to your cause. They can't tell you to go away if it's an open meeting, and there will already be media people assigned to it. Hold a press conference on the lawn outside just before the meeting starts, or simply pass out written material explaining the problem (you'll find some ideas on how to run a press conference in the appendix). Only your imagination limits you. A word of warning, however—in using this strategy your goal should be to create a bit of attention for yourself, not to dominate the meeting or divert attention completely. Dominating a slightly related public meeting may lose the audience's sympathy for you, and it infuriates the people in charge, thereby violating the prime rule of survival in the public arena: make no unnecessary enemies.

Make It a People Story

I learned how to make people stories the hard way. Several years ago we scheduled a press conference to attack insurance companies for the way we felt they were price gouging nonprofit agencies. Two things surprised us. First, some reporters actually showed up. Second, one of the television guys wanted to do a story on the subject on the six o'clock news and asked us to send him to some nice visual location where something terrible had happened because of the insurance people.

The setup was perfect—Big Bad Insurance Company versus Innocent Day-Care Center—but we had spent so much time collecting facts and figures to prove our case that we had never heard the real stories. As soon as he realized what had happened the reporter was gone, and so was our opportunity. Moral: Virtually everything you want the media to look at has to be framed as a story about real people and real conflicts.

It's no accident that international disarmament treaties and cease-fires get played out as stories abut the individual statesmen who negotiate them rather than as the results of complex historical trends and global politics that they are. If the state is planning to build a prison twenty-five paces east of your barbecue pit, you've automatically got the people angle. But if the matter is, say, uncontrolled condominium conversions, be prepared to talk about Mrs. Renter being forced out of her twenty-five-year lease, not about population drift across metropolitan statistical areas.

Give It a Name

No matter how sexy your story or how well you inspire coverage, you will never reach people effectively until you can describe your cause in a single word or phrase. Although it isn't absolutely necessary, a title that tells what you're all about in addition to giving you a recognizable identity is perfect. One of the most effective naming jobs I ever saw was done by a welfare advocacy organization that took some statistics showing that people receiving public welfare are forced to live below the government's own poverty level and turned them into a campaign called "Up to Poverty." You didn't need to be a bleeding heart to understand how bad off people were if poverty looked like up to them.

Make up Some Snappy Quotes

Nothing carries a story like one or two great quotes. Have you noticed how newspapers and television stations always have the same people commenting on the same issues? They're not necessarily the best experts around, just the most quotable. How you say something is more important than what you say. If you're worried that you can't think on your feet well enough to get quoted, write up a press release ahead of time. Many print reporters will be just as happy to snatch a press release and get out without even speaking with you (believe it or not, many reporters are shy, and even if they're not shy they're busy). Besides, few reporters can turn down an article that's already half-written.

Do the Reporter's Work for Him

The hardest part of a reporter's work is often sorting through a blizzard of facts without any overall concepts for guidance. By doing the reporter's work for him or her, you not only produce a set of facts that hang together, you subtly suggest a framework within which any future investigation might continue. The reporter is free to reject your ideas, of course, but their sheer existence will be hard to ignore completely.

Some public figures, frequently those targeted by the media, believe that reporters are fundamentally lazy. As a sweeping generalization, this is a misreading of both a reporter's scope and the role of the editors. For a variety of reasons, the reporter's scope of potential subjects is so broad that he or she usually has little choice but to accept the conclusions of experts in the field rather than conduct extensive independent analysis. And the reporter's willingness to dig deep into a subject is really just a function of editorial direction and the economics of their outlet.

The wisest thing that nonprofit executives can do is to forcibly demystify the media for themselves and their staff. As a system for delivering a product it can be affected by executive behavior just as readily as any delivery system. With a bit of planning and foresight, it can actually turn into an ally of strong programming.

CHAPTER 22

A FEW WORDS ABOUT LOBBYING

Let's get down and dirty for a moment, shall we? Let's talk about power. Fainthearted readers, move on—this won't be pretty.

In the past, it has been fashionable, or at least permissible, for nonprofit administrators to hold what I call the Dog Germ Theory of Politics. Entering the political arena for these folks traditionally has been on a par with getting licked on the mouth by a dog—indescribably disgusting, somehow unhealthy, and certainly not the kind of activity in which one voluntarily engages.

This is unfortunate, because all nonprofit organizations need some amount of political power with which to carry out their mission. In this country, there are only two sources of power—money and people. One of the places where these two power streams frequently collide is the legislative process. Today's entrepreneurial nonprofit executive knows that part of the job is being comfortable in that environment.

Can, Should

Some nonprofit leaders and board members believe that tax-exempt organizations are prohibited from getting involved in political affairs under any circumstances. Not exactly. Public charities may not engage in political campaigns on behalf of a given individual for elective or appointive office. This is an out-

233

right ban, no questions asked. But they can engage in lobbying on behalf of issues as long as it is not substantial.

The part giving rise to legal and government careers is the definition of "substantial." There was always a great deal of uncertainty about what the term "substantial" really meant. For years, nonprofit corporations as well as the IRS itself had operated without a clear-cut understanding. No one was particularly happy with the situation. In response, in 1976, Congress enacted section 501(h), which provided, for the organization choosing it, a precise arithmetical test for compliance as measured by percentage of exempt purpose expenditures (churches, private foundations, organizations engaged in testing for public safety, and certain other organizations cannot choose section 501[h]). In 1990, after a protracted period of rule writing and rewriting, the IRS issued definitive regulations governing section 501(h).

The stakes remain high for the nonprofit engaged in potentially extensive lobbying, since the ultimate penalty can be loss of tax exemption. However, under the formulas spelled out by section 501(h), excessive lobbying in the short term leads only to payment of a special tax on the amount calculated to be over the formula. While no one likes to be taxed on an expense, the "lobbying tax" is far from onerous and for some organizations will simply be a cost of doing business.

Head for Gucci Gulch

The real limitation of consequence on nonprofits' lobbying activities comes from the splitting of lobbying into two parts, direct and grass roots. The latter is capped at 25 percent of the total direct lobbying expenses that can be incurred without the lobbying tax kicking in.

As a limitation on lobbying effectiveness, this is ingenious. The kind of direct lobbying that most nonprofit organizations are going to be able (or willing) to do has no room for the slick, Gucci-shod lobbyist troops of popular mythology. Yet it is the inside players who have the greatest influence in direct lobbying. The one time the sides might be somewhat even is when the money of the insiders is offset by the sheer volume of the people outside. But to arouse sufficient numbers of people to legislative action requires a massive grass roots effort—precisely the kind limited by section 501(h).

Still, it can be done. More important, it *should* be done. With government contributing such a solid chunk of many nonprofits' revenue, and with that same government controlling so much of the policy relating to what other nonprofits are dedicated to doing, there really isn't much question about getting involved with that ol' devil politics. So spend the next few minutes arming yourself with the proper information.

How

Start with legislators. The thing to remember about legislators is that they are just like you and me. This is a frightening prospect.

In the last few years it has become fashionable to deride legislators as corrupt, arrogant, incompetent, and just about any other negative attribute one can imagine. Not only is it fundamentally dishonest to suggest that the simple act of seeking or holding a public office brings out these characteristics in greater degree than other forms of human behavior, it misses the larger point. Public scorn for lawmakers is one way of controlling them, some of the other ways being low salaries, poor working conditions, and the ballot box itself.

The fact is that no single legislator can concentrate on more than a few areas of interest at a time. If one assumes prior employment as a rough guide to legislators' interests, and if legislators roughly parallel the employment patterns found in the population at large, about one of every twenty-five legislators will have worked for a nonprofit corporation. Considering the wide variety of nonprofits and missions, the chances of meeting a legislator who has anything remotely resembling an intimate familiarity with your type of nonprofit's issues is close to nil.

Worse, the first struggle with many legislative types may be to clear away myths and misunderstandings. One newly hired executive director I know arranged a meeting with the local state senator and the state senator's aide, who happened to be a long-time acquaintance. In the middle of the director's tale of money troubles, the aide suggested that the center help solve its financial problems by not paying stockholders a dividend that quarter. It was then that the mental health administrator realized what an enormous education job lay ahead for him.

The Rule of the Four S's

Before you run off to meet with your local lawmakers, consider what it is that you would have them do. It is easy enough to believe that the legislative meeting is the message, that simply getting word to one or two legislators is sufficient. If the process of arranging a meeting was at all challenging, it is particularly tempting to believe that the real work was done. However, at that point it has just barely started.

Other than listening well, the lawmaker can only do four things. These limited functions have nothing to do with a particular lawmaker's individual talents; they are inherent in the legislative process. Here are the four things, in descending order of importance:

SAY
SIGN
SEE
BE SEEN

Like many things about politics, the positions of "say" and "sign" above seem backward. What could be more important than legislators signing things, especially letters of support and bills? Taking "sign" as another term for "vote," what could be more important than legislators' votes?

It's a reasonable objection, but it overlooks the true nature of the legislative process. The final vote is the end point, not the beginning. Legislative bills represent change, and the function of a legislature is to slow down change and make it more manageable whenever it is inevitable. The proper prelude to a proposal for change is talk—lots of it. Lawmaking bodies are most comfortable when a proposal for change gradually makes its way from wacky idea to marginal consideration to serious proposal to law. Along the way it gets stretched, chopped, shaped, and squeezed into a form as unthreatening to the status quo as the force behind the proposers will allow. Those negatively affected by the proposal have ample opportunity to derail it or, failing that, to plan for its possible acceptance months or years in advance.

The single most important thing a piece of legislation can have going for it is a committed and consistent legislative champion. What that champion says about the bill to his or her colleagues is far more important than anything he or she might sign. One of the intriguing aspects of the legislative process is that there is usually a fair amount of trust among lawmakers about the technical provisions of a bill. Those who have spent their time developing expertise in some area can be respected and relied upon for interpretations of what a bill means and what it might do were it to become law (support of the bill is another matter, however).

The third most important thing lawmakers can do is to see things. Often, the thing they see is information. One government official I know used to say that he wrote reports for fifty people. He routinely circulated them to hundreds if not thousands of people, but his real audience was about fifty people placed throughout the executive and legislative branches of government. The tough part for him was to figure out which fifty people should read each report, and then actually get them to read it.

Another thing lawmakers see is problems and solutions. Of all the people in government, lawmakers are in the best position to see problems firsthand and to focus attention on successful solutions. To the extent that your program represents a successful solution, it is in your interest to get lots of legislators out to see it—*now*, before it's necessary. When I was a lobbyist, one of our most successful programs was our "Have a Legislator for Breakfast" campaign. The idea was to invite local representatives or senators to an actual nonprofit agency to see how things worked, and to get them to do it first thing in the morning before they even reached their office and heard about the day's crises.

Finally, lawmakers are on the job in order to be seen. Their sheer presence at meetings, hearings, and rallies conveys a message even if they do not speak a word. Being seen in the right places nurtures an image of power, which is to say it nurtures power itself. Sheer physical proximity to centers of power and influence is enough in most cases to create a strong reputation. The entrepreneurial nonprofit executive picks a legislative champion by where he or she stands—in more ways than one.

How Public Hearings Are Like a College Education

A public hearing on a cause is like a college education for an individual. Without it, a cause is likely to go nowhere, but having it guarantees nothing.

Think of public hearings as legislative theater in which you are both the actors and the audience, at differing times. (For practical guidance, see Tips on Testifying in the Appendix.) Your job is to figure out when you are being asked to be which. To understand what this means, ask yourself a single question while planning your testimony: Do you believe that no one on this committee has ever heard of the general problem you are about to describe? Unless your cause is very narrow and has few implications for the world at large—in which case a new law is probably not the best way of fixing it—you can bet that at least some of the legislators know exactly what you are talking about and may have even made up their minds on it.

So what are you doing at a public hearing talking about something your listeners already know? The answer is that you are in the first stages of what Franklin Roosevelt reportedly told a group after they finished making an articulate plea for some reform or other. He agreed with them completely, he said, but trying to put it in place at that point would be political suicide. Their job, he explained, was to go back out and force him to do it.

At any legislative hearing, whether it's on a specific bill, a budget proposal, or simply on a general topic of interest, the game gets set up like this before anyone even speaks:

They know there is a problem (none of you would be there if there weren't).
You know that they know there is a problem.
They know that you know that they know there is a problem.

While appearing to talk to each other, what you are both doing is talking, with varying degrees of earnestness, to a third party. Sometimes that third party is neatly represented by the media, but more often no real third party is actually there so it takes the form of a more or less understood presence.

Almost always, the legislative response to a hearing will be to do nothing and do it graciously. For the time being, that is acceptable, since testimony at a hearing can do little more than tie a cause to a balloon to float it up into the public debate. Go home—you did your job well.

Rallies and Demonstrations

In case anyone missed the point at the hearing, you might want to have a rally or two. It's great fun, and for anyone who grew up in the '60s or early '70s it can be positively nostalgic. All you really need is a giant mailing list and/or an advertising system, some cardboard signs, one or two good speakers, and a parade permit.

In truth, rallies and demonstrations are effective more for what they do for participants than for any immediate effect they are likely to have. Other than voting in periodic elections, rallies and demonstrations are one of the best ways for ordinary people to do something concrete in the service of a particular cause. Rally sponsors can benefit from an intensive internal focus for a concentrated period of time, as well as from the opportunity to identify organizational strengths and weaknesses. They can also help in myriad other ways, ranging from free publicity to the chance to update member mailing lists.

The problem with rallies and demonstrations is twofold. First, precisely because everyone is doing them, they are less effective. In order to be successful, a rally or demonstration needs to be much bigger or somehow more outrageous than all of its recent predecessors. If you want to know how big or how outrageous it has to be, talk with whomever provides security for the targeted building. If they are ho-hum about your plans, rethink the approach.

As with all attention-getting devices, they are also subject to circumstances beyond your control. If Kansas City has an earthquake the day of your rally, throw away your press releases; you won't find any takers (throw away your geology textbooks while you're at it). Once we planned a statehouse rally for three months and drew three thousand people—the biggest crowd at the statehouse for the previous two years—but because a top administration official happened to be getting grilled by a legislative committee that day, we got a brief mention on page twenty-seven instead of the larger play the event might have drawn otherwise.

The bigger problem with rallies and demonstrations, however, is that they are a public admission of powerlessness. They signal a kind of outsider status that can easily be ignored should lawmakers choose to do so. Powerlessness is like poverty—noble under certain circumstances, but not to be desired when there's a job to be done. Still, it's possible to run an effective campaign based on rallies and demonstrations and often nonprofit organizations find themselves having to do that anyway. The key is to capitalize on the outsider status as *the* issue, thereby turning it into an us versus them contest. There are a lot more of uses who feel powerless than thems who feel powerful, so the strategy can produce a big win.

If the Minutemen Had Formed a Task Force, We'd Be British Today

Sooner or later in your advocacy for your cause, it will happen: someone in a position of authority will ask you to be on a task force. Push your cause for long enough, and it's practically inevitable. A task force forms every seventeen seconds in this country, so you need to be prepared for when it strikes near you. With tongue only slightly in cheek, here are some rules of thumb for task force participation and management.

The power core of any task force is equal to or less than the square root of its membership. I don't have the slightest idea why this is true, but I have seen enough task forces to know that it is about as escapable as the law of gravity. In any group of ten, no more than three people hold the true power, in a group of twenty-five it's held by five or fewer, and so on. What this means is that you can write off at least 75 percent of any task force membership when it comes to influencing future directions. Go for the power core and forget about the rest.

Three notes on this principle. First, we're talking about the power to get something accepted, not the power to veto. Veto power is the easiest kind to get. Everyone has it from time to time, especially when everyone is more or less as powerful as everyone else, but it is essentially a defensive tactic upon which you cannot build. Second, the power core is subject to maximums only, not to minimums. The truly powerful in any group can number anywhere from zero up to the square root of its membership. Third, over the long run, rank or status outside the group is not necessarily indicative of power within.

You can tell the power core members by their behavior at meetings. They tend to do one of three things: they rarely attend a meeting (too boring, and they're busy with more important things), or they attend and never pay attention (why bother—they already know what's going to happen), or they attend and pay excruciatingly careful attention to everything everyone says (Ivy League breeding).

The half-life of any task force membership is a maximum of six months. A concept from nuclear science expresses a fundamental rule of task force life cycles. A task force loses one half of its potential active membership every six months or less. Theoretically, this process can go on just about forever if the original task force is large enough, but in practical terms most task forces are done within a year of inception.

This is the reason why smart task force leaders never oppose individual new members proposed at the beginning. They know that as long as the suggestion isn't totally outlandish, the chances are excellent that the individual will fade away or at least never penetrate the power core.

The best predictors of success in a task force are the presence of paid staff and paid-for photocopying. No one seriously expects a corporation, nonprofit or for-profit, to accomplish its goals without adequate resources. Why do we think task forces are any different? A task force without adequate resources to carry out its job is just a social club.

Often, though not always, the members of a task force are the ones who bring the resources. Sometimes, the task force convenor contributes the dollars and/or staff time. In any event, the source is less important than the presence of the goods. What is most important of all is that someone, preferably a group of someones, takes the task force seriously enough to part with some cash or real staff time in order to make it work. Contributing real resources is the most critical symbol a participant can produce.

A successful task force report is like a Christmas tree. A successful task force report is a little like the old-fashioned Christmases where each child gets to put an ornament on the tree and can point with pride to his or her contribution throughout the season. Rarely does a task force produce a new idea; ordinarily it synthesizes already suggested ideas in its own special way and gives voice to those which may have been suggested but overlooked before. As an interim step with no power to implement anything, the task force is a kind of laboratory in which to experiment with various options to see whether they really ought to be allowed out in society. The member who pushes an idea through the process and into the task force report is putting his or her own ornament on the tree.

The task force as Christmas tree also tends to neutralize the disaffected member's only trump—resignation. Since the architecture of a task force is its most powerful feature—if you're not there you don't get to hang an ornament—the resignation of any member is of great interest to friend and foe.

The disaffected task force member planning on playing his or her trump card needs to recognize its limitations. First, no one will put you on any future task forces on the chance that you will do it again (admittedly, this may make it appealing). Second, to be most powerful, it has to be done with at least one other person. Crackpots don't travel in pairs, so multiple quits shift the implied burden of explanation mainly onto the people who put the task force together. The town manager where I live once fired a twelve-year Wetlands Protection Commission member for sleeping during a site inspection (or maybe it was for staying awake). Within a month, five of the six other members also quit, and suddenly the town manager was on the defensive.

Finally, resignation must be done with great public fanfare. Call a press conference if there are enough media around that might be interested. Write letters to the local papers. Invite yourself to appear on local radio or television interview shows. Once the attention starts coming, be sure your complaints are the issue, not you personally. Use such phrases as "for the good of . . ." and "in good conscience . . ." and "could not allow myself to be. . . ." With the right spin, you'll end up looming like a tower of right-mindedness over that pip-squeak of a task force report.

Lobbyists and Other Despised Minorities

If there is a profession not involving illicit drugs that ranks closer to the bottom of public esteem, I can't imagine what it is. Lobbyists are widely regarded as the cause of everything from bloated government to premature hair loss. After two decades of lobbyist bashing, the Gucci-shod, French-tailored, carefully coiffed, middle-aged white male with cash in his briefcase has found a place in popular mythology.

Style questions aside, the entrepreneurial nonprofit executive knows that there is a place for lobbyists in today's management. While most lobbying for nonprofits is done through trade and professional associations, there are times when the freestanding nonprofit will need a lobbyist's services. Whichever way it happens, the two functions of a lobbyist are the same.

The Right Stuff at the Right Time

The primary job of a lobbyist is to get the right information to the right person at the right time. One aspect of this role is to provide legitimate information. What is hardest for the uninformed citizen to comprehend is just how much policymakers in government rely on lobbyists' information. Obviously they know that the information will be tailored to the lobbyists' purpose, although sometimes the information used is so basic as to be hard to slant.

To guard against intrinsic bias, most legislative and executive staffs develop a tacit discount index for each lobbyist, discounting from 1 to 99 percent of what they are told. It is a cumbersome process, but rarely does a legislative staff have enough research capacity to respond to every request, so it is a necessary trade-off. Also—and this part should never be overlooked—sometimes the staffs *agree* with the lobbyist.

The second aspect of lobbyists' information goes to the heart of the policymaker's motivation. One professional lobbyist I know says that lawmakers' motivations can be summarized in the rule of FGH—Fear, Greed, and High Principle. How lobbyists use the second piece of this trilogy is already well discussed. Less well known is how lobbyists can play up or help arrange voters' anger at a legislator's record. And even less well recognized is the fact that many legislators do cast principled votes, at least whenever the absence of the first two states gives them the option. In fact, in my experience it is the legislator's own version of High Principle that serves most often as the guide to a voting decision, unless one of the first two interferes.

Holding all of this together is the lobbyist's own knowledge of the process, both parliamentary and political.

Little Brother Is Watching

Underlying the lobbyist's second role is what my friend Judy Meredith calls a fundamental law of politics: Lawmakers make different decisions when they think they're being watched. Not better decisions, necessarily, just different. It is the lobbyist's job to convey to each lawmaker the fact that, on a particular vote or issue, his or her constituency is watching closely. A lobbyist I used to work for had a natural advantage in this category. With a full head of snowy white hair and a face that looked permanently sunburned, he would sit like an avenging angel in the visitors' gallery every time there was an important vote. The message was hard to miss.

Still, the more powerful message that someone is watching comes not from lobbyists but from constituents. There really is no substitute for constituent-to-legislator contact. Every letter and telephone call communicates a message of sunshine more articulately than an army of lobbyists. The legislator may not vote the so-called right way as a result of it, but at least he or she will know that there may be a price to be paid for rejecting the message.

CONCLUSION

In the past few years there has been much discussion about "profit-making ventures" and alternative sources of funding for many types of non-profit organizations. Across the country there has been a collective stirring in the field as individual agencies pursue specific projects designed explicitly to imitate their for-profit counterparts. For the most part, this development is entirely positive, but it bears a heavy irony. Projects that are ultimately successful are often regarded as unique, slightly miraculous and unequivocally *different,* this last perception reinforced by the haze of unfamiliar legal and tax terminology that the projects often must create.

This aspect of the new concern for profits can be dangerous if it diverts our thinking away from the fact that the entrepreneurial leadership that makes a nonprofit organization's for-profit venture a success is the same that is needed to make traditional nonprofit programs a success. Entrepreneurial non-profit leadership is a product of the mind, not the tax code. It consists primarily of challenging the restrictive and self-defeating assumptions that have traditionally dominated this field in order to create opportunity for all involved with the organization. It extends to virtually every aspect of the executive's role and, performed successfully, it invigorates and rejuvenates any organization.

The wholly entrepreneurial nonprofit executive is a rare breed, and should be. He or she pushes the frontiers of our knowledge about the field, a role always better suited for a minority class.

247

But if few are capable of being full-blown entrepreneurial non-profit executives, virtually everyone can learn to be more entrepreneurial in smaller ways ranging from fundraising practices to dealing with employees.

In the preceding material, I have tried to describe some of the ways in which any nonprofit executive can become more entrepreneurial in the pursuit of his or her institution's mission. More important, I have tried to show how any nonprofit executive can begin to *think* entrepreneurially within the context of the traditional nonprofit organization. This book was written with firm belief in the necessity and vitality of this field. It can be judged a success many years from now if it has had a role in making its own title a redundancy and the ideas it presents delightfully quaint.

PART IV
APPENDIX

APPENDIX 1

SAMPLE ASSOCIATION HEALTH INSURANCE PLANS

Many associations offer some form of health insurance program for member groups. Here are some broad-based associations with health plans.

State Associations:

California Association of Nonprofits
P.O. Box 1478
Santa Cruz, California 95061
408/458-1955

Center for Nonprofit Corporations
36 West Lafayette Street
Trenton, New Jersey 08608
609/695-6422

Colorado Association of Nonprofit Organizations
1245 East Colfax, Suite 411
Denver, Colorado 80218
303/832-5710

Delaware Coalition of Agencies
613 Washington Street
Wilmington, Delaware 19801
302/652-3991

Health & Welfare Council of Central Maryland
22 Light Street
Baltimore, Maryland 21202
301/752-4146

Washington Council of Agencies
1001 Connecticut Avenue, N.W., Suite 925
Washington, D.C. 20036
202/457-0540

National Associations:

American Society of Association Executives
1575 Eye Street, N.W.
Washington, D.C. 20005
202/626-2751

The Society for Nonprofit Organizations
6314 Odana Road, Suite 1
Madison, Wisconsin 53719
608/274-9777

APPENDIX 2

HOW TO RUN A PRESS CONFERENCE

Pick a day. Wednesday is the best day for new media stories. The long weekend crowd has finally filtered back, the story grinders have used up the weekend backlog, and the week's quota of variety is beginning to look a bit thin to the assignment editors. Since the Supreme Court announces its decisions on Monday, they can't ambush you, and the stock market has had a chance to get a grip on itself if one was necessary. Thursday starts to look like the weekend to some readers and viewers, and smart public figures try to release bad news late Friday. Check a regional or national paper to make sure that no federal or local agency is going to release major economic statistics that week.

Pick a time. Generally, the earlier the better because reporters get backed up or diverted to late-breaking stories as the day goes on. He who asks the question wins the argument, so if you have any opponents they'll have to spend the rest of the day responding. The alternative, especially for very local stories involving local media, is a nighttime press conference and since there are usually only one or two local papers interested in your subject you'll look like you should have had it in a telephone booth. On the other hand, don't make it too early, or the press won't cover it. Mid- to late morning is usually a good time.

Don't cancel it. We once scheduled a press conference for the early afternoon of a day that saw a large and unpredicted snowstorm. Being thoughtful types, we canceled the event that morning in order—we thought—to get a chance at better coverage the

253

next time. What we failed to see was that everything else was getting canceled too, which meant that the six o'clock news that night was going to have a lot of time to fill with shots of reporters standing beside snowy roads (they don't do those stories because they like them, you know).

Furthermore, because we had told them generally what the press conference was going to be about, some reporters had already made plans to include the material in later broadcasts. Because we canceled, many of them not only had to come up with a last-minute replacement for our story but they also had to trudge around in the snow to get it. One of them solved the whole problem by pretending it didn't exist. As I watched the evening news that day, the anchorman's voice smoothly assured viewers that "at a press conference held today, it was announced. . . ."

Rehearse the presentation. The value of rehearsing your presentation is the same as those college entrance examination courses—you may not score higher, but at least you'll know what's coming. A press conference isn't a chance to claim a share of your fifteen minutes of fame, it's an opportunity to get your message across to a lot of people you otherwise couldn't reach. Rambling, uninteresting speeches don't grab anybody, and unless you are a very disciplined, experienced public speaker it's rambling you'll be.

When you rehearse the session, ask a friend or two to sit in. Have them sit in the equivalent of the front row and tell them that their job is to ask as many hostile and negative questions as they can think of. Negative reporters often sit very close to their subjects—being physically close tends to put subjects off balance and rob them of any sense of protection (at the press conference itself, reporters selecting front row seats may be a signal that tough questions are on the way). Rehearsing this way should prepare you for the toughest parts, as well as help you eliminate the irrelevant.

More than four is a bore. Resist the temptation to hold Brady Bunch press conferences. After working so hard on a campaign, there is an understandable tendency to want to trot out the mother of the issue, the father of the issue, its sisters, brothers, aunts, uncles, and second cousins, but that will only dilute the focus.

One way to counteract this self-defeating phenomenon is to look for people who can fill three or four readily identifiable and separate roles—spokesperson, technical expert, typical victim, etc.—and confine the speaking parts to them.

People trump words. Words trump numbers. It's practically impossible for electronic media reporters to make a story from words or numbers alone, and print media types don't want to if they can avoid it. People will carry the story much better than a splendidly written press release or a few sheets of official-looking statistics. On the other hand, you do need the balance that a well-substantiated argument laid out in words and numbers can give you, so it's a question of the proper balance. If numbers are unavoidable, use charts, preferably in color, and never use a sheet of paper with columns of numbers on it unless you highlight two or three specific amounts.

Visuals trump everything. If there is a cardinal rule in any form of communication, it is this: don't *tell* your story, *show* it. Television is only interested in things that move around or are inherently dramatic, and television tends to set the news agenda in a local market. Visuals can be anything from a powerful speaker to a real person epitomizing your issue or even colorful pictures and graphics. Television and newspapers may want to reproduce the latter themselves if the story seems interesting enough, or cameras may want to linger on them as background shots for a reporter's voice-over.

Give them something to take home. Be sure to hand out at least a few pieces of paper summarizing what was presented. Reporters feel cheated if they don't take something away, and having written material prepared ahead of time gives you the advantage of a lasting presentation of your message. Be certain that what is said in writing fits exactly with what was said at the press conference, or follow-up attention may get focused on the wrong area. Have the name and telephone number of a contact person at the top of the release for further questions.

APPENDIX 3

TIPS ON TESTIFYING

Arrive early. Some hearing planners insist on previous written sign-ups, others take testimony on a first-come, first-heard basis. Arriving early insures that you will be in the best position to press your case for a few minutes no matter what happens.

Choose your seat according to your strategy. Public legislative hearings are no place for self-effacement. If your job is to promote your cause personally, sit front and center at eye level with the panel chairperson. Play the odds and sit slightly to the chairperson's left, since most people's line of sight actually veers slightly to the left.

If your role is to observe and analyze, sit so you can see all panel members' eyes and as much of the audience as possible. Organizers should stand at the back of the hall if permitted, or at least near the doors for quick exit and reentry.

Use buttons. If you will have a substantial number of colleagues at the hearing, have some buttons with a catchy slogan made up ahead of time. Make sure they are bright enough to be recognized at a distance, and get them to your colleagues before they enter the hearing room.

Arrange speakers carefully. If you have any chance at all to influence the order of speakers, grab it. The press will leave within an hour unless it's something very special or a slow news day. It sounds counterintuitive, but get your strongest message up-front in each speech, and get your strongest speaker first. Make sure each speaker has something different to say—after a while, even supporters get turned off by a steady stream of duplicate testimonies.

Tell them what you do. Assume no one understands what it is you do or why you are there, and find a way to explain both in forty-five seconds or less.

Use props. Photographs, charts, graphs, and just about anything else related to your testimony give panel members relief from a steady flow of information presented verbally, highlight your message, and can be a great visual for newspapers and television. And it doesn't need to be slick. One advocate I know presented a handwritten poster that was so effective the legislators were still talking about it three years later.

Hand in written testimony. Always bring enough written copies of your testimony for every panel member plus committee staff, if any.

NOTES

Chapter 2

1. Leo Troy, *Almanac of Business and Industrial Financial Ratios* (Englewood Cliffs, New Jersey: Prentice Hall, 1990).

Chapter 4

1. Mary Hall, *Getting Funded: A Complete Guide to Proposal Writing* (Portland: Portland State University, 1988).
2. Susan E. Kalish, *The Proposal Writer's Swipe File: 15 Winning Fund-Raising Proposals* (Rockville, Maryland: The Taft Group, 1984).
3. *The Non-Profit Times,* July 1990.

Chapter 7

1. James Kouzes and Barry Posner, "What Followers Expect from Their Leaders," *Management Review,* January 1990.
2. Peter F. Drucker, "What Business Can Learn from Nonprofits," *Harvard Business Review,* July-August 1989.
3. "Challenges for the 1990's," *The Chronicle of Philanthropy,* January 9, 1990.
4. Peter F. Drucker, "What Business Can Learn from Nonprofits," *Harvard Business Review,* July-August 1989.

Chapter 8

1. C. K. Prahalad and Gary Hamel, "The Core Competence of the Corporation," *Harvard Business Review,* May-June 1990.
2. Bruce Kirchoff, "Who Survives," *Inc.,* July 1988.

3. Peter F. Drucker, "What Business Can Learn from Nonprofits," *Harvard Business Review*, July–August 1989.

Chapter 12

1. American Institute of Accountants, *Internal Control: Elements of a Coordinated System and Its Importance to Management and the Independent Public Accountant*, 1949, p. 6.

2. American Institute of Certified Public Accountants, *Report of the Special Advisory Committee on Internal Accounting Control*, 1979, p. 11.

3. Robert N. Anthony and David W. Young, *Management Control in Nonprofit Organizations, Fourth Edition* (Homewood, Illinois: Irwin, 1988).

4. James L. Heskett, *Managing in the Service Economy* (Boston: The Harvard Business School Press, 1986).

5. Lecture by Professor I. Morgan, Boston University.

Chapter 17

1. Kathy Kolbe, *The Conative Connection* (Reading, Massachusetts: Addison Wesley, 1991).

2. *The Non-Profit Times*, December 1990.

INDEX

261

ABOUT THE AUTHOR

Thomas A. McLaughlin has nearly twenty years of nonprofit management experience, including many years as an executive with two major Massachusetts social service agencies and as Associate Director of the Massachusetts Council of Human Service Providers. Currently he is a senior consultant in the Division of Tax Exempt and Governmental Services in the Boston office of the accounting and consulting firm BDO Seidman. He is also on the management faculty of the Boston University School of Social Work, and is the nonprofit business columnist for the *Boston Business Journal*. He holds Masters degrees in Business Administration and Urban Affairs, and he lives with his wife Gail Sendecke and their two children in Wilmington, Massachusetts.